COMING: THE END!

Russia & Israel in Prophecy

COMING: THE END!

Russia & Israel in Prophecy

THOMAS S. McCALL
ZOLA LEVITT

ISBN: 0-8024-4007-X

1 3 5 7 9 10 8 6 4 2

Printed in the United States of America

To
the people of Israel

"I will bless them that bless thee"
(Genesis 12:3)

Contents

Foreword to the 1987 Edition

No generation since the early years of the Christian church has had more reason to turn to the prophetic Word than those living in the twentieth century. In keeping with prophecy, Israel has moved back to her ancient land. Initial steps toward a world church and a world religion have already been taken. Many observers of the political scene believe that, in order to avoid nuclear suicide, all nations must unite into one world government.

With Israel back in her land and Russia boasting about having the greatest army in the world, Ezekiel 38 and 39 become extremely relevant. Those two chapters predict an invasion of Israel from the north and provide a setting for the fulfillment of prophecies concerning the end time. Though scholars differ in their interpretations, a likely scenario is that Israel will be basking in the supposed safety of a peace treaty during the first half of the last seven years preceding the second coming of Christ. Though Israel is not at peace today, the coming world ruler is destined to give Israel her longed-for peace at the beginning of his political career. Anyone desiring to know God's program for the end time will be interested in what the Bible predicts concerning Russia. This book will challenge the student and enlighten the scholar.

JOHN F. WALVOORD

Preface to the 1987 Edition

More than a decade has passed since we first published *The Coming Russian Invasion of Israel* in 1974. What a decade it has been in further preparation toward the war Ezekiel prophesied. Think of the events that have transpired:

Middle East manipulation of the world economy through the embargo and then overproduction of oil

The Iranian revolution (Shah ousted; Khomeini installed)

The Ethiopian revolution (Selassie ousted; Communists installed)

The Iranian hostage crisis

Israeli bombing of Iraqi nuclear plant

Israel-Lebanese war (vast caches of Soviet arms found in PLO warehouses)

Libyan and other notably Syrian-backed terrorism, Western military retaliation

Russian invasion of Afghanistan, Soviet gateway to the Middle East

The key figures of Ezekiel's prophesied war keep moving inexorably toward their great moment of destiny, without knowing that the Bible predicted their postures millennia ago. The Soviet Union continues to supply the enemies of Israel, such as Syria and the PLO, with money and arms. Iran (Persia) is embroiled in a debilitating war with Iraq. Ethiopia has been transformed through revolution from one of Israel's best friends in Africa to one of her worst enemies. Libya, under the radical leadership of Colonel Qaddafi, has fomented terrorism against every form of "Zionism" in the world, and has only recently pulled back its claws in response to U.S. military retaliation. The near neighbors of Israel—Lebanon, Jordan, and Egypt—have been somewhat neutralized through war or treaty. Only Syria remains as a determined enemy among Israel's immediate neighbors. Now Syria is being isolated as a terrorist state by England and other Western powers. The Middle East, because of its vast reserves of oil, continues to dominate the world's economy.

What can we say about all these developments? Shall we ignore them prophetically and consider them interesting geopolitical movements and nothing else? Not if we believe the Bible!

God, the great revealer of the future to Ezekiel and the other prophets, is obviously allowing all these things to occur so that the predictions in His Word may come to pass. The coming Russian invasion of Israel and the subsequent War of Armageddon are not pleasant things to write about, and we take no pleasure in describing the prophetic cataclysms ahead. Our only consolation is that these events are indications that the rapture of the church must be ever closer to fulfillment and that the glorious return of our Lord Jesus Christ to the earth to establish His long awaited kingdom must be coming sooner than many think.

We commit this little volume into the hands of our Lord that He might continue to use it to bring many to the realization of the truthfulness of His Word and the greatness of His salvation.

Preface to the First Edition

The world today is like a bomb with a lighted fuse. Conditions everywhere indicate that it is only a matter of time before the bomb is ignited and a global upheaval takes place.

The Coming Russian Invasion of Israel is a warning of the approaching explosion. Like a man who sees flames enveloping a building and cries, "Fire!" the authors sound an alarm.

It will not be surprising, then, that many will regard the authors as alarmists. In a sense, of course, that is exactly what they are. But when there is a real danger (and there is), anyone in his right mind appreciates being warned.

In the pages of this book there is not one note of false alarm. The coming catastrophe outlined is real. It is based upon that which is declared by God Himself in His eternal Word.

Biblical prophecy sets forth the future of Russia with dramatic clarity. Her invasion of Israel at the end of this age is incisively predicted in the Bible as clearly as the regathering of the Jews and their establishment as a present-day nation of Palestine.

This treatise on prophecy, though popularly written, constitutes a reliable guide to what is going to happen in the world in the near future. It will benefit everyone who reads it. The Christian will be strengthened in his faith in God's Word. The non-Christian will see his need of Christ's salvation to prepare him to face impending world catastrophe.

MERRILL F. UNGER

Introduction

This book has been exceedingly difficult to write because the events the authors intended to "predict" kept virtually coming to pass during the writing.

The authors are not the prophets, of course, but Ezekiel and other Bible writers who foresaw the coming Russian invasion of Israel have become so timely that it is difficult to set down interpretations of their prophecies before the events actually happen.

When we began this project in the summer of 1972, the idea of Russia's invading Israel was a matter of the future, though many recognized it as a possibility. But in the fall of 1973, during the writing, the Yom Kippur War broke out in the Middle East, and the American military went on "Alert," apparently fearing a Russian invasion of the combat area.

When the authors speculated, in 1972, that the oil of the Middle East might become a vital issue of world affairs, we didn't dream we would be waiting in line for gasoline in Texas a year later!

As we print this book as a third update now in 1992, there are those who say that the Russian threat is dead. But we believe Ezekiel's prophecy will yet be fulfilled and that one day, sooner or later, Russia will make its move against Israel and all that the prophet foretold will come to pass.

This book is more than timely. We believe that it is a grim necessity to warn the world, believers and unbelievers alike, that the biblical messages about today's world affairs are relevant and imminent. The coming Russian invasion of Israel is not far off, and it will profoundly affect us all.

Since 1948, when Israel was revitalized, the Arab world, Europe, and the superpowers have all been engaged in an escalating confrontation about the Jewish state. Russia has emerged as the major enemy of Israel over that time. We believe, with Ezekiel, that Russia's animosity will not be satisfied short of an invasion.

Although this particular development has surprised the world, it comes as no surprise at all to students of the Bible. For 2,600 years, the Russian invasion of Israel in the end times has been common knowledge to readers of Ezekiel.

The format of this updated book has the new chapters interwoven with the original chapters. Thus, the original chapters (with some editing) are 1-4, 9, 12, 14, and 15. On the other hand, the new chapters are 5-8, 10-11, 13, and 16.

Our new readers, who have never read the original book, will probably want to read the book straight through. Those who have already read the original may wish to concentrate on the additional information in the new chapters.

As in another one of our books, *Satan in the Sanctuary*, we have taken a single issue of Bible prophecy and have attempted to illuminate it completely in the light of current events. This time we have had to constantly revise the manuscript to keep up with ongoing developments. We felt, at times, that we might be too late. That may yet prove to be true.

But if you have this book in your hands before the Russian invasion of Israel, please know that the alarms sounded here are real. Ezekiel and the other prophets have been right too many times for the world to ignore them any longer.

And this issue is serious. It is truly a matter of life and death.

As we watch the coming Russian invasion of Israel in preparation, we pray that many thousands of readers will put their trust in the true Author of prophecy, the Lord Jesus Christ, and that believers in Christ will redouble their efforts to proclaim the redeeming Word of God while there is still time.

Until the coming Russian invasion of Israel, "The truth shall make you free" (John 8:32).

T. S. McCall
Zola Levitt

1

The Russians Are Coming

Russia is going to attack Israel.

Had anyone said that fifty years ago, it would have seemed a perfectly impossible idea, the way things stood.

But the prophet Ezekiel said it 2,600 years ago.

Ezekiel 36 to 39, which we will examine in detail, is one of the Bible's "histories of the future." It chronicles, by means of symbolic visions given to the ancient prophet, the coming Russo-Israeli war. It discusses the actual battle campaigns and the outcome, as seen by the war correspondent Ezekiel.

This event is not to be confused with Armageddon, the "war to end all wars." The Bible also foresees that ultimate conflict, but the Russo-Israeli war is to precede it.

Ezekiel places his prophecy in the end times. The Bible repeatedly refers to this final period of earthly history when God's plan for our world will culminate. It will not be a happy time. It is commonly called the Great Tribulation. And it seems to be coming up very soon.

Biblical descriptions of the end times include a host of issues quite familiar to readers of today's newspapers. Jesus, whose second coming is to climax the Tribulation Period, warned His disciples about the strife and tension, false prophets, famines, earthquakes, and national conflicts that have now become the world's daily bread. He said, "Nation will rise against nation," and He told of "wars and rumors of wars" (Matthew 24).

There is not adequate space here to consider all the prophecies about the end times and apply them to our world situation.[1] Suffice it to say here that the world today has all the requirements to satisfy Ezekiel's gruesome visions of the Russo-Israeli war and mankind's most comprehensive achievement of self-destruction, Armageddon.

Past ages could not hold a candle to us for weaponry, attitude, and the general know-how of destroying one another. The world has always had war, but our thermonuclear capabilities, international tension, and disregard for human life make us the best contenders ever for the honor of receiving the One who said sadly, "Unless the Lord had shortened those days, no one would have been saved" (Mark 13:20).

If there is to be global war, we are the ones who can do it.

But first, the Russians are coming.

Ezekiel sees a massive land invasion from the far north into the Middle East. The Scriptures urge upon us that Russia will be the nation to mobilize an enormous land army that will cross the Caucasus Mountains, Turkey, Syria, and Lebanon to attack Israel. It's David and Goliath again, and again a question of the faithful against the pagans.

And again God takes quite an interest in the affair and sides with the underdog.

The outcome of the war is given: Russia meets her Waterloo. "Behold, I am against you, O Gog," says God. 'You shall fall on the mountains of Israel, you and all your troops, and the peoples who are with you; I shall give you as food to every kind of predatory bird and beast of the field. You will fall on the open field; for it is I who have spoken,' declares the Lord GOD" (Ezekiel 39:1, 4-5).

The concept of a huge land army vanquished upon the open field is still very much a part of our modern warfare, automated as it is. We are going to discuss Russia's rationale for a march to Israel and the unique circumstances that will come about to satisfy the prophecy.

THE SICKLE AND THE SCIMITAR

For Ezekiel, to foresee an alliance between Russia and the Middle Eastern nations was going out on a limb. The pagan Middle East was, in his time, a most advanced civilization, the world's center of scientific knowledge and refinement of culture. It had dominated the Mediterranean for a period longer than from Christ to the present. Its magnificent architecture, religions, and military might were acknowledged and respected throughout the civilized world. But Russia, so far as anybody knew, was inhabited by roving bands of virtual cave people.

But look at the way things are now. Russia is a tremendous power. The claws of the bear have reached out in all directions from that vast frozen land, and Ezekiel is getting more believable by the day.[2]

The Arabs have become mere middlemen now as Russia advances upon the true cradle of civilization, the Holy Land.

In late October 1973 the American military went on "Alert" in an announced response to Russian troop movements. It was said that Russia was planning to move combat troops into the theaters of the Yom Kippur War.

Some said the maneuver was purely a political gambit, but the important thing was that nobody was really surprised. For Russia to attack Israel would not be at all out of line with current developments.

That's never been true before. Until the present day, nobody except Ezekiel ever thought that Russia would attack the Holy Land.

But in the past forty-five years Russia has increasingly become Israel's archenemy. She has armed the Arabs. There has been an enormous outlay of men and matériel for war steadily flowing to the Arabs from the Soviets, amounting to one of the most fearsome military mobilizations in history. Along with the death machines come talented Russian technicians to teach modern vengeance to the Arabs, who have no lack of vengeance in their own right.

Some of those Arab soldiers put on their first pair of boots one week and learn to use a rocket launcher the next. But the knowledge and the equipment keep piling up.

Israel Sees Red

Israel does not regard the Arabs as the real enemy, wisely enough. When you're shot with a Russian-made AK 47, you might as well give credit where it is due.

General Moshe Dayan, hero of the 1967 Six-Day War, has stated flatly, "Israel is now at war with Russia."

The Arabs have their much-touted reasons to fight—they claim that the Jews took their land, they don't belong there, and so on. But the real issue here is the continuing power of Russia (the Magog to the extreme north) against Israel, the revived homeland of the Jewish people scattered throughout the world.

That is how Ezekiel saw things. Through him God named the real combatants—the enemies of God versus the friends of God.

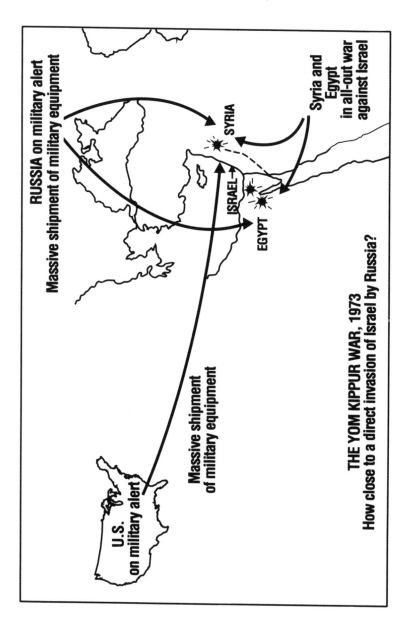

RUSSIA on military alert
Massive shipment of military equipment

Syria and Egypt in all-out war against Israel

SYRIA

ISRAEL

EGYPT

Massive shipment of military equipment

U.S. on military alert

THE YOM KIPPUR WAR, 1973
How close to a direct invasion of Israel by Russia?

NOTES

1. Hal Lindsey, *The Late Great Planet Earth* (Grand Rapids: Zondervan, 1970), and Thomas McCall and Zola Levitt, *Satan in the Sanctuary* (Chicago: Moody, 1973) give more complete discussions of end-time prophecies.
2. For further information, see *Russia: Imperial Power in the Middle East* (Jerusalem: Carta, 1971).

2

The 4,000-Year Tragedy: Ezekiel the Prophet

The crowds must have really come out when Ezekiel held forth. His was a rare kind of ministry. He was a walking, talking example of national tragedy, demonstrating by his own sufferings what was to befall the nation of Israel. God told the Jews, "Thus Ezekiel will be a sign to you; according to all that he has done you will do" (Ezekiel 24:24).

It was a tough assignment. Patient Ezekiel, thought by some to be insane, endured an unrelenting series of personal tragedies and afflictions. He was a one-man show—a living drama of disaster.[1]

He shut himself up in his home, bound himself, and was struck dumb. He was ordered by the Lord to lie on his right side for 390 days and then on his left side for 40 more days, by way of demonstrating to Israel the number of years of her iniquity.

His food and water were rationed by God, and he was charged to eat disgustingly unclean bread, "having baked it in their sight over human dung" (4:12). He lost his wife but was not permitted even the consolation of mourning.

And that wasn't the half of it.

His suffering still goes on, in a way, because his majestic book is probably the least known and least heeded of the Bible prophecy books. With all of his painful efforts, his messages seemed largely lost on the ancient Jews—and on us too.

It's time to give this unsung hero his due. We're about to see the fulfillment of his boldest, most dramatic visions reenacted by whole nations rather than by one lone man of God.

He was one of the prophets of the Exile, the period when the majority of the Jewish nation was detained in Babylon in the sixth century B.C. King Nebuchadnezzar of Babylon had taken his place somewhere in the middle of the list of those tyrants of history with solutions to "the Jewish problem." He had laid siege to Jerusalem, examined his prisoners—an entire civilized nation—and simply carried off all but the poor and indigent.

In the bargain, he acquired some of God's key men. Ezekiel and the brilliant Daniel were among the captives. Jeremiah, whose clear-eyed forecast of this very disaster proved accurate to the letter, was left behind with those not worth deporting.

We can gather that the Jews were permitted to function within their traditions while detained, since the prophets went about their work. From the confines of ancient Babylon, Daniel and Ezekiel were able to see events of our own times and beyond. It is fair to say that they were able to see the end of the world as we know it.

Ezekiel's visions confounded his audiences, and they still leave the casual reader mystified. But as world events progress, we have the advantage of seeing the pieces fall into place. It would have been a lot to ask of the unhappy prisoners of Nebuchadnezzar to picture a mighty Russian army swarming down on Israel. But that is not nearly so hard to picture nowadays. Ezekiel is rapidly coming into fashion.

He begins his story of what we are calling the Russo-Israeli War with a typically bewildering vision of a valley filled with dried bones. God takes Ezekiel into this grisly scene to make a point. The prophet describes his conversation with God:

> And He said to me, "Son of man, can these bones live?" And I answered, "O Lord GOD, Thou knowest." (37:3)

You can't blame him for hedging. Erekiel must have been as baffled as we are.

God ordered Ezekiel to speak to the bones—to say to them, "O dry bones, hear the word of the LORD" (v. 4).

Some preachers today complain about speaking to "dead" audiences!

Ezekiel did as he was told, prophesying to the dead bones that they would live, that God would restore them with new sinews, flesh, skin, and breath.

The situation has been immortalized in the spiritual "Dry Bones." "Dem bones gonna walk aroun'," says the likable tune accurately enough. Ezekiel reports, "So I prophesied as He commanded me, and the breath came into them, and they came to life, and stood up on their feet, an exceedingly great army" (v. 10).

The meaning of the vision is revealed by God in the ensuing passages:

> Then He said to me, "Son of man, these bones are the whole house of Israel; behold, they say, 'Our bones are dried up, and our hope has perished. . . .' Therefore prophesy, and say to them, "Thus says the Lord GOD, 'Behold I will open up your graves and cause you to come up

out of your graves, My people; and I will bring you into
the land of Israel.'" (vv. 11-12)

The vision teaches the regathering of the Jews back
to Israel from the "graveyards" of the Gentile nations.
This part of the prophecy is easy enough to understand for anyone living after A.D. 1948 when the Jews truly were regathered to their Promised Land. It wasn't quite
as easy to appreciate for those living in the long nineteen
centuries between the destruction of the second Temple
of Jerusalem (A.D. 70) and 1948, during which time the
Jews were dispersed and without a homeland.

To put Ezekiel and the end times into perspective,
we should say something about the four-thousand-year
tragedy that is the history of the Jews.

The Jews have had a special destiny since the day
God made His covenant with Abraham (Genesis 12).
They became for all time the chosen people. This status,
though ultimately a profound blessing and privilege, has
had its ups and downs. Because of the Jews' very special
responsibility to God, they have constantly enjoyed, or
suffered, divine interest in their affairs.

That is not just a theological viewpoint. History
bears out the distinctive joys and deep despairs of this
chosen people.

Tevye, the poignant Jewish protagonist of *Fiddler on
the Roof*, cajoles God, "Why don't You choose somebody
else for awhile?" A look at the story of Judaism explains
his discouragement.

The Jewish nation, as a political entity, really began
with the enslavement in Egypt. With the great Exodus
from slavery led by Moses about 1500 B.C. the Jews were
given a land promised by God. There followed almost a
thousand years of autonomy, peace, and the building of
an intellectually and scientifically enlightened civilization in Israel.

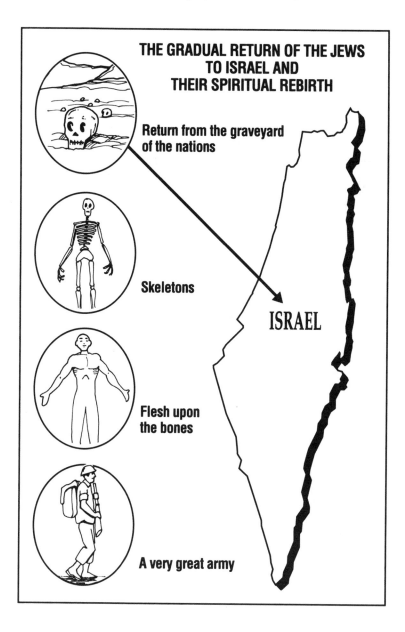

**THE GRADUAL RETURN OF THE JEWS
TO ISRAEL AND
THEIR SPIRITUAL REBIRTH**

**Return from the graveyard
of the nations**

Skeletons

**Flesh upon
the bones**

A very great army

ISRAEL

The high point of that reverent and politically successful millennium was the middle of it, when the Jewish nation progressed to world importance under the leadership of David and Solomon. The brilliant King Solomon achieved the great ideal of God and the Jewish people when he constructed the magnificent Temple of Jerusalem.

There followed, however, a decline in the Jews' reverence for God. The prophets constantly warned the people—God had full charge of this nation and would act according to its faith.

Speaking in worldly terms, pagans to the north were gaining strength and military skills, and the Jews, relaxed in their now well-established and successfully defended kingdom, failed to heed the signs of the times.

When the prophet Jeremiah frantically sounded the alarm—actually naming Nebuchadnezzar of Babylon and the Chaldees as the near-future invaders—the government was unimpressed. In fact they were so annoyed that they jailed the prophet to quiet his clamorings.

About the only individual who thought Jeremiah had something to say was Daniel, who faithfully studied the older master's conclusions about the predicted Babylonian exile. God gave Daniel the incredible prophecy of the seventy weeks, in which he foresaw the advents of the reclaiming of Israel, the first coming of the Messiah, our own times, and even the future return of Christ.

Ezekiel was at that time carrying out his own difficult assignment among the captives and looking ahead to the far-future Russo-Israeli war.

The Jews were released from Babylon by the conquering Cyrus of Persia, as prophesied by Isaiah and Jeremiah, and once again they put their amazing nation-building powers to work.

By 516 B.C. they had established the second Temple in Jerusalem, and they proceeded though a shaky five centuries as a passive little country coexisting with Persia, Greece, and Rome.

They held on while Alexander the Great and numberless other pagan conquerors traded the known world back and forth, until the times of the Roman Empire.

Rome had a Russia-like knack of gathering territory, either quietly or with the sword, and a bottomless appetite for taxes. By the time of Christ, the Jews were exceedingly uncomfortable with their divided loyalties—their faith went to God, but their worldly produce went to Rome. They plotted rebellion.

That was a very bad idea. In a worldly way, they had no chance whatsoever in a war against Rome; spiritually they were in a state of extreme disobedience to God—they had rejected their Messiah.

They got together a national rebellion just after the time of Christ, in A.D. 66, and Rome dealt with it unmercifully. In the final siege of Jerusalem and the battle for the Temple site, the Jews suffered more than a million casualties in five months.

Only Hitler could rival such easy accumulation of Jewish bodies. The Jewish nation took more losses in that final campaign than the United States has suffered in all of her wars since 1776.

But the most unkind cut of all was the destruction of the second Temple. The Romans were so thorough that Jesus' prophecy was completely fulfilled; not one stone was left upon another.

But the depleted little nation staggered on. It's very hard to picture what a society is like when one out of every three people formerly functioning is dead. But the Jews somehow pulled their society back together and went on, heavily taxed and strictly policed by their Roman masters.

By the time of the emperor Hadrian, about A.D. 130, they were thinking rebellion again. There had been several skirmishes through the years, with heavy Jewish losses, and war on a national scale was in the offing. Hadrian provoked the Jews by building a pagan temple on the Jerusalem Temple site and forbidding or restricting many of the Jewish religious practices. He gave the Jews credit for Christianity—a charge they hardly appreciated. He was clearly trying to obliterate the very idea of Judaism, and he almost succeeded.

The war in A.D. 135 was actually a guerrilla operation in which the Jews fought like the Viet Cong; they spread the rebellion out over the whole of the country, picking at the Romans with endless small campaigns and ambushes. The enemy obliged with a nationwide mop-up.

The Jews were plainly too difficult to rule; the tedium of constant policing, the recurring combat, and the detested monotheism steadily emanating from Jerusalem finally tired the Romans, and they threw the Jews out of the land.

Thus began the great dispersion of the Jews that lasted until 1948.

There are no times of joy to report from that long period. Somehow the Jews, still faithful to their religious practices wherever they happened to be, never got themselves back together. From the days of Christ on, the Jews have had steady heartbreak.

The whole world now became the enemy of Judaism. Somehow, no one could let the vanquished Jews just rest. They were slaughtered like animals during the Inquisition. They were starved and murdered endlessly in forced conversions throughout Europe. Persecution followed them to the ends of the earth.

Russia was no exception. The Jews suffered terrible pogroms and conversion-by-starvation. The present Soviet restrictions on Jewish emigration continue the tradition.

And finally Hitler came forward to attempt the complete extermination of the Jews.

That, at last, gave the world a bad conscience about the chosen people, and they were once again permitted their Promised Land.

The events since 1948 are within memory and show little slackening of the typical troubles for the Jews. The Arabs are following in the footsteps of the cruel Egyptians of antiquity; the Russians are getting up steam as Babylon did.

Now we turn to prophecy to know the future of Israel. Ezekiel will take us on from here.

From surveying Jewish history, we can better appreciate how much meaning there is in this "dry bones" vision of Ezekiel. "Can these bones live?" Can a people dispersed without a common culture for all those centuries ever pull themselves together again? Can dead things come back out of graves and be restored to their ancient land?

Only by an act of God.

> "Then you will know that I am the Lord, when I have opened your graves and caused you to come up out of your graves, My people. And I will put My Spirit within you, and you will come to life, and I will place you on your own land. Then you will know that I, the Lord, have spoken and done it," declares the Lord. (37:13-14)

Note

1. See Charles Lee Feinberg, *The Prophecy of Ezekiel* (Chicago: Moody, 1969), p. 224.

3
Brinkmanship:
Ezekiel the Political Analyst

Here comes the part we were telling you about.

Ezekiel now analyzes the coming Russian invasion of Israel. Chapter 38 introduces "Gog of the land of Magog, the prince of Rosh, Meshech, and Tubal" (v. 2), and says of them, "And you will go up, you will come like a storm; you will be like a cloud covering the land, you and all your troops, and many peoples with you. . . . And you will come from your place out of the remote parts of the north . . . a mighty army" (vv. 9, 15).

The names "Gog" and "Magog" are a bit cryptic, but it is not difficult to trace just who is meant here. Serious students of the Bible had identified Russia with these names long before she achieved her present supremacy. The *New Scofield Reference Bible* states, "The reference is to the powers in the north of Europe, headed by Russia . . . the attempt to exterminate the remnant of Israel in Jerusalem."[1]

It is fascinating to compare the note to this passage found in the old Scofield Bible, annotated in 1909 during the Czarist age of Russia. The brilliant commentator C. I.

Scofield could not have foreseen either the rise of Russia to world importance or the regathering of the Jews to Israel in 1948, but he says, "That the primary reference is to the northern (European) powers, headed up by Russia, all agree. . . . The reference to Meshech and Tubal (Moscow and Tobolsk) is a clear mark of identification. Russia and the northern powers have been the latest persecutors of dispersed Israel."[2] Scofield's reasoning has been kept intact in the latest edition, with only the deletion of the word "dispersed."

The genealogy of biblical names is a study in itself and beyond our scope here. *The Late Great Planet Earth* gives a clear background in the chapter "Russia Is a Gog," pointing out that the terms of Ezekiel 38 first appear in Genesis 10.[3] They are actually names of sons and descendants of Noah, and it was the custom for tribal, and finally national, names to evolve from original founders' names. Apparently the tribal name Magog moved northward from the Middle East. Josephus, a Romanized Jewish historian of the first century, notes that Magog is called the Scythians by the Greeks. Secular history books trace the fierce Scythian people, who lived in the northern regions above the Caucasus Mountains, as forerunners of modern Russia.

But even without all of that, we can still clearly see the Bear of Russia through the geographical hints given by Ezekiel. He stresses three times over that this mighty enemy of Israel comes from the "remote," or "remotest," "parts of the north" (38:6, 15; 39:2). The Hebrew gives the qualifier meaning "extreme" or "uttermost" to the term "north" all three times. And of course, the ultimate power to Israel's uttermost north is Russia, the nation most likely to succeed in being "a cloud to cover the land."

Furthermore, we have "Gog" identified as the "chief prince" of the invaders. The Hebrew phrase translated "chief prince" is *nesi rosh.* The word *rosh* can be an adjective meaning "head" or "first," but it could just as easily be a place name, "Rosh." The Hebrew lexicon of Brown, Driver, and Briggs indicates that Rosh here is the proper name of a people.[4] It seems that Ezekiel's Rosh has become today's Russia. That is more than a hint. God indeed stands at the door and knocks.

And lastly, we have Meshech and Tubal, compared by Scofield and many others to Moscow and Tobolsk, militarily industrialized citadels of the future enemy. Moscow, as a matter of fact, lies due north of Jerusalem.

Russia by herself would be sufficient as an enemy, or, as the Jews sing on Passover, "*Dyenu!*" (enough for us). But Ezekiel specifies that there will be some allies as well.

Persia, Ethiopia, and Libya are given, clearly enough, and also Gomer and Beth-togarmah (38:5-6; Togarmah, KJV*). The latter two names pertain to Eastern Europe (the former Iron Curtain countries) and southern Russia, respectively, as we shall see. The former names have come down to us intact except for Persia, which is now Iran.

Curiously, Egypt is not mentioned among the antagonists. Will something happen to Israel's perennial enemy before the conflict? Will she not be important enough to merit listing among the allies at that time? Will the name Libya automatically include Egypt by then?

Persia, or Iran, would make a first-rate ally for Russia in a land invasion of Israel. Its location and terrain would greatly facilitate troop movements. Given the large scale of the invasion foreseen by Ezekiel, the mountain ranges separating Russia from the Holy Land become a factor; and those in Iran are more hospitable than those in Turkey.

* King James Version.

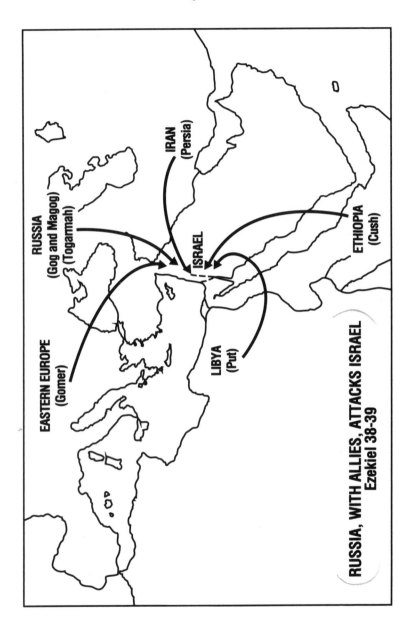

RUSSIA, WITH ALLIES, ATTACKS ISRAEL
Ezekiel 38-39

The Elburz mountain range in Iran is not so extensive as the Caucasus in Turkey. The rest of Iran is generally more accommodating than hilly Turkey, too. And the advancing Russians could create something of a pincer effect if they arrived from two directions against Israel.

Ethiopia may represent more than the country that bears its name. Its ancestry is traced to Cush, a grandson of Noah (Genesis 10), whose descendants apparently migrated southward into all parts of Africa. The Organization of African Unity, founded in 1963 in Addis Ababa, was described by Ethiopian emperor Haile Selassie as "a single African organization through which Africa's single voice may be heard."[5]

Libya's role is becoming more of a typecasting every day. It is easy to see that this advancing Arab power would be most receptive to participating in hostilities against Israel. It has ever been a nation typical of the Arab mentality and way of life, and it is presently arming. Giving some idea of how Libya is pressing Ethiopia to work against Israel, a 1973 *Time* magazine report of a recent summit meeting of the Organization of African Unity says,

> Potentially the most divisive was a demand by Libya's Muammar Gaddafi for an all-out condemnation of Israel, and a break in relations by every O.A.U. state. Ethiopia and 26 Black African countries maintain diplomatic ties with Israel; Lybia, the O.A.U.'s five other Arab members and seven Black African nations are violently anti-Israeli.[6]

Gomer "and all his bands" is a reference to the countries of the former Soviet bloc in Eastern Europe. Northward migrators who settled along the Danube and Rhine rivers, Gomer's descendants are traced through the ancient Cimmerians back to Genesis 10.

Beth-togarmah is a reference to the area of southern Russia or Armenia and adds an interesting note to the method of invasion. The area is the origin of the Cossacks and is well known for its fine horsemen and its cultivation of superior cavalry forces. Ezekiel pictures horses being used in this invasion (38:15), and this very issue has been used many times to try to invalidate the prophecy. After all, who's going to ride a horse into a mechanized twentieth-century battle?

Those critics were silenced during the Korean War when the Red Chinese, no mean horsemen themselves, moved huge numbers of troops in mountainous terrain by that tried and true method. The invasion of Israel involves mountainous terrain.

In any case, these last two allies, Gomer and Beth-togarmah, complete the picture of the invading force. Israel is virtually surrounded. The Mediterranean Sea is at the west of the Holy Land, and the invading allies will come from the north, south, and east.

It makes so neat a geopolitical picture of a logical coming invasion that it is almost too perfect. Perhaps we cheated a little, looking at the current scene and bending the prophecy to fit it?

Actually, the placement of the allies was researched and decided by Bible students long before the Iron Curtain takeover of Eastern Europe, before the independence of Israel, before the rise of Russian Communism, and even before the alliance of distant nations was considered militarily feasible. The Hebrew lexicon of Wilhelm Gesenius, written in the early 1800s, gives an analysis from which we do not differ.[7] Imagine what the scoffers thought back then!

THE CURRENT SCENE

We should go around the protagonists once more with a view to what they are doing on the current scene. Students of Ezekiel have never had a better opportunity to appreciate his foresight, and time may be running out.

First, Israel. Ezekiel beautifully pictures modern Israel with a few pointed remarks. He talks about the inner mountains of Israel "which had been a continued waste" (38:8). True enough, until the present era, Israel's fruitful mountains were constantly desecrated by foreign occupiers. The Muslims dammed up the rivers of the lush Sharon Valley and made it a marshland in order to deter invasion. The forests of the little country, always dependable, were destroyed by occupying Turks, who unfeelingly cut down the magnificent cedars to build temporary structures.

The "land of milk and honey" was made almost into a desert.

King Solomon maintained a building program that was the envy of the ancient world, with largely domestic materials. But when the Jews got back their land in 1948, they had to first plant trees and restore natural irrigation in order to have wood. "Plant a tree in Israel" was the worldwide plea of the Jews in the 1950s, as schoolchildren sent their dimes to the Holy Land to restore it.

But a few verses later, Ezekiel pictures an improved land:

> And you [Gog] will say, "I will go up against the land of unwalled villages. I will go against those who are at rest, that live securely . . . to capture spoil and to seize plunder, to turn your hand against the waste places which are now inhabited, and against the people who are gathered from the nations, who have acquired cattle and goods, who live at the center of the world . . . to carry away sil-

ver and gold, to take away cattle and goods, to capture great spoil." (38:11-13)

That was quite a mouthful in Ezekiel's time. Who had ever heard of a land of unwalled villages back then? A wall to those ancient reckoners was what we call national defense today. The image shows how futuristic was the thinking of the prophet. And then we see that the invader, when he gets to "the desolate places that are now inhabited," will fall upon a people "that are gathered out of the nations." That must also have sounded strange to Ezekiel's audience; the Jews were not nomads, to say the least. Since they had a promised land, emigration was virtually a sacrilege. True, they were detained in Babylon because of military invasion, but Israel was still Israel. For the Jews to leave their land was to turn their backs on God. How could the prophet even speak of Jews as being gathered out of other nations?

Only an Ezekiel or a Daniel or an Isaiah—those possessed with the secret information given by God—could begin to picture the extent of Israel's coming exile.

Finally, in his statements about what the invader will encounter, Ezekiel depicts a successful nation, where the people "have gotten cattle and goods," and where silver and gold are there for the capturing.

What do these things symbolize? What does Israel have today that Russia would want?

Well, first there is very real wealth in Israel. The country is small but enjoys a vigorous economy. The people have a Japanese-like enthusiasm that continually makes something out of nothing.

Then there is wealth in terms of raw materials. Little oil has been found there, but the mineral deposits of the Dead Sea, persistently defying extraction, represent a great prize. There is a wealth of brains, too. Russia gobbled up tremendous amounts of scientific and industrial know-how when she took over in Eastern Europe, particularly in East Germany.

We must keep in mind that invasions are not what they once were. When, for example, Nebuchadnezzar or the Assyrians accomplished an invasion, it was hard to tell a country had been there when they started. The new look in takeovers is much more discreet. The invading country attempts to leave intact all that might be useful to it—factories, farms, universities, laboratories—and have it all functioning on the invader's behalf. Ideally, the invader would like to just run up his flag on the flagpoles and leave everything else as it is.

The Russians are masters here. Occasionally they have "used the teeth on a knot that would not yield to the tongue," but they have by and large taken over vast amounts of the world with great discretion. Eastern Europe still functions; it has just been working for the Reds. Where ideology would not work, they have employed tanks, but in any case the countries and their people end up as second-class Russians.

Israel is a fine target for this kind of thing. She's the prize of the Middle East.

And finally, perhaps most important, Israel has a prime location for the orderly spread of Communism.

It is said that three things are important in real estate —location, location, and location. That applies whether you are buying the real estate or stealing it. Israel's location is of prime importance to Russia.

Looking on the world globe, one can see that Communism has enjoyed a steady, organized expansion emanating from Russia. It has gone to the Pacific on the east, the Berlin wall on the west, and to the frontier of the ice on the north. To the southeast it has penetrated Indochina with some difficulty. To the southwest—Israel's direction—it has jumped over some territory and penetrated in Africa and the Middle East. Israel stands right in the jumped-over spot.

Israel represents an outpost of democracy standing directly in the way of the Communist expansion. She would provide a most convenient base from which the Communists could operate in the Middle East and Africa. She has good access by land and sea to those areas. Her harbors and airfields are among the best. The liability of the long supply line that has frustrated invaders from Alexander to Napoleon to Hitler would be eliminated in this sector if Russia could control Israel.

Ultimately, the oil of the Middle East might go to the great power close enough to grab it. The oil embargo proved how effective an economic and political weapon oil can be.

We have seen Russia establish outposts and then proceed from them to control vast territories. The situations in the Balkan and Ural countries led ultimately to the takeover of Eastern Europe. Operations from North Korea and North Vietnam were more troublesome but cost the free world dearly to contain them.

A foothold in Israel for the Russians would obviously mean trouble for everybody else.

Ezekiel's view of the spoils available seems conservative in view of the present scene.

Looking at the allies of Russia in the coming conflict, we can see that Ezekiel's stage is not completely set as yet—at least not at this writing.

Iran is not officially aligned with Russia at the moment, though such an alliance in the future would not be surprising. Ethiopia is not aligned with Russia either at the present writing, though for some years her leaders were in the Russian camp.

Libya is another matter. Some time ago she acquired fifty Mirage fighter jets from France, and she has learned how to use them (by trial and error). She has become an influential power with Egypt; indeed she may well supersede Egypt by the time of the invasion. Talk of a merger between the two nations is constant.

Libya's increasing importance in the Arab bloc, along with the fading of Egypt, may account for the lack of mention of Egypt in the prophecy. There has been a shift recently to Libyan predominance in that sector. Although Ezekiel's listeners could have easily understood the participation of Egypt in an invasion of Israel, he omitted her and mentioned Libya. Will Egypt decrease as a major power among the Arabs by the time of the invasion? Will Libya be the key antagonist from that sector?

The northern allies are already dressed for their roles. Gomer (Eastern Europe) could probably be counted on by Russia to act on cue. Beth-togarmah is literally part of Russia and may justify Ezekiel's unique picture of a horse-soldier invasion.

When will the invasion come?

We cannot know, even with today's insights, the times and seasons of the Father, taught Jesus, but we can watch the signs of the times and interpret them. We mentioned some of the signs of our times that qualify this present generation to be the one living in the end times, or "the latter days." That term, utilized by Ezekiel in this prophecy (38:16; see also 38:8, KJV), was also used by Jesus in His message about wars and rumors of wars. It is fair to say that all of our various circumstances might repeat together in some future time. But we would be remiss not to recognize the high correlation between the prophecy of Ezekiel and others and the characteristics of our age.

Historically, few people ever really took the prophets seriously. That was a very bad habit we should now break. With the restoration of Israel and the rise to world importance of Russia, Ezekiel's once-confusing messages take on a new urgency.

We have looked at the details of the Russian alliance and the present scene. Before we go on, we might do well to briefly review relations between Russia, the Arabs, and Israel. Are those nations really setting up for a major conflict at this time? Could Ezekiel have meant our generation? What about God's view? Israel is His chosen people.

In God's view, taught Ezekiel, this coming conflict is really a war between the atheists and the godly. The Arabs, sons of Ishmael and Muhammad, are virtually godless in the biblical view, and the Russians are outspokenly atheistic. The Jews, however far from their Messiah, are the worshipers of God in this conflict and will be able to count on His promises, in the prophet's view.

During the last forty-five years we have seen an ever-growing antagonism between the citadels of atheism and the Promised Land. When Israel was restored to the Jews, it brought up a feud that goes back four thousand years to the dispute between Isaac and Ishmael. The divine blessings and vast real estate holdings of their father, Abraham, were in question then.

They still are.

For nineteen centuries things were quiet between Jews and Arabs, while the Jews were dispersed throughout the world and the Arabs came and went as they pleased in Palestine. But Semites have long memories. When the Jews returned forty-five years ago, they considered that they were getting back their land—the land promised to them by God.

The Arabs considered Israel (Palestine) to be their own ancestrally given property.

They might have worked something out, but Russia, hovering over the argument like a spectator at a prize fight, preferred the hostile atmosphere.

For her part, Russia at first thought Israel might be some sort of socialistic outpost in the Middle East, and she recognized the new state diplomatically in 1948. The original Israeli leaders, veterans of the kibbutzim—which resemble the Russian collective farms in some ways—seemed to embrace certain socialist concepts. But it was quickly seen by Russia that the new country was to be nothing like the materialistic, atheistic homeland of Communism.

The honeymoon ended very soon. Israel set up a kind of socialism that allowed for enormous concern for the individual human life, strong ties with theistic convictions and the Jewish heritage, capitalistic enterprise, and great political diversity. That was obnoxious to Russia.

Fissures appeared steadily in the relations between the two countries, until it was clear that the Russians preferred the company of the Arabs in the Middle East.

Three actual wars occurred—in 1956, 1967, and 1973—with Russia fully allied with the Arabs. Some propaganda about Russia's helping the Arabs recover their cherished land was published each time, but the pretenses have cleared up now. It's now plainly a matter of land-grabbing and the spread of Communism.

The wars helped show Russia and the world that the new little nation was no patsy. The Jews were reminded of the great days of King David, when invading armies confronted Israel only at their extreme peril. The war of 1967 demonstrated Israel as a power to be reckoned with. The world looked on in astonishment as the Jews vanquished the Russian-armed Arabs in just six days.

There is now relentless rhetoric about renewed hostilities, and fickle Russia still waits on the sidelines, armed to the teeth and making alliances. It appears she's just picking her moment.

These last forty-five years argue forcefully for Ezekiel's predictions coming to pass very soon. He gave no inkling of a lengthy period of brinkmanship but gave his analysis of the invasion in quick chronological sequence after the restoring of the Jews to their land.

Due to the strange dramatic manifestations of God's Word by the prophet, some people thought he was crazy But he does not look crazy now.

Look now with Ezekiel at the actual Russian invasion of Israel.

Notes

1. *New Scofield Reference Bible* (New York: Oxford, 1967), pp. 881-82 n.
2. *Scofield Reference Bible* (New York: Oxford. 1909), p. 883 n., Scofield's parens.
3. Hal Lindsey, *The Late Great Planet Earth* (Grand Rapids: Zondervan, 1970), p. 63.
4. Francis Brown, S. R. Driver, and Charles A. Briggs. *A Hebrew and English Lexicon of the Old Testament* (Oxford: Clarendon, 1959), p. 912.
5. "Decade of Destiny," *Time*, June 11, 1973, p. 44.
6. Ibid.
7. William Gesenius, *A Hebrew and English Lexicon of the Old Testament*, trans. Edward Robinson (Boston: Crocker & Brewster, 1854).

4

From Russia with Blood: The Invasion of Israel

"I am against thee, O Gog," says the Lord at the beginning of Ezekiel 39; "I will turn thee back, and leave but the sixth part of thee" (vv. 1-2; both KJV).

In this stirring section, the prophet depicts in vivid detail the defeat of the mighty invader of the north and the terrible results of the war. "The sixth part" seems to refer to those spared of the vanquished Russian land force; this 84 percent casualty rate is unheard of in modern warfare.

It is hard to understand this severe defeat except as an act of God, which is what Ezekiel says it is. It accomplishes the purposes of glorifying God before Israel and the world and of finally restoring much-chastened Israel to its God.

Interesting details of the combat and its aftermath are revealed in this chapter. Some have raised controversies of interpretation, but the overall picture is distressingly clear.

Apparently Russia is overwhelmed early in her campaign, virtually at the moment of the invasion. We see no lengthy scenes of battle, and the attackers will "fall on the mountains" (v. 4) and "fall on the open field" (v. 5). The invasion does not appear to affect population centers, and we hear of no destruction of Israel. Shades of the Six-Day War!

We are given only a hint of this supernatural conquering of a militarily superior force. Ezekiel quotes God: "I shall strike your bow from your left hand, and dash down your arrows from your right hand. . . . And I shall send fire upon Magog" (vv. 3, 6). The allies of the invader are disposed of as well! "You [Gog] shall fall . . . and all your troops, and the peoples who are with you" (v. 4).

Fire falling upon a land army is not nearly as difficult to imagine in this age as it was in Ezekiel's time. Napalm or even nuclear detonations might well be described in that way. But this is a matter of speculation. In the preceding chapter, Ezekiel supplies more details, quoting the Lord: "I shall rain on him [Gog], and on his troops, and on the many peoples who are with him, a torrential rain, with hailstones, fire, and brimstone" (38:22).

John F. Walvoord says, "Some natural questions are raised about this. Some have suggested that the description of hailstones, fire and brimstone might be Ezekiel's way of describing modern warfare, such as atomic warfare. There is a possibility that Ezekiel was using terms he knew to describe a future situation for which he did not have a vocabulary. The language of Scripture indicates, however, that the victory over this invading horde is something that God does. It is God, Himself, who is destroying the army."[1]

Ezekiel goes into quite a bit of detail about the aftermath of the war. Enough is left for scavenging birds and animals: "I shall give you as food to every kind of predatory bird and beast of the field" (39:4). The dead bodies of the invaders apparently will strew the fields and mountains of the holy land: "For seven months the house of Israel will be burying them in order to cleanse the land" (v. 12).

That lengthy burial detail will occupy a lot of people: "Even all the people of the land will bury them" (v. 13), and some will find full-time employment at it: "And they will set apart men who will constantly pass through the land, burying those . . . left on the surface of the ground, in order to cleanse it" (v. 14).

With typical Israeli civic pride and endeavor, they will sterilize their Promised Land. Even travelers through the land—tourists—are to be asked to watch for stray remains and to mark the spot for the burial details: "And as those who pass through the land pass through and anyone sees a man's bone, then he will set up a marker by it until the buriers have buried it in the valley of Hamon-gog" (v. 15). "Hamon-gog" is the Hebrew for "The multitude of Gog," which is to become the name of this vast cemetery for the invaders.

This grim and morbid information about the burial emphasizes the very large size of the invading force and the totality of its defeat. But even more of a testimony to this will be the burning of the weapons that fall from the hands of the combatants. Ezekiel specifies that seven years will be involved in the burning of the weapons of this vast army.

"Then those who inhabit the cities of Israel will go out, and make fires with the weapons and burn them . . . and for seven years they will make fires of them" (v. 9). That has a practical side: "'And they will not take wood from the field or gather firewood from the forests, for they will make fires with the weapons; and they will take the spoil of those who despoiled them, and seize the plunder of those who plundered them,' declares the Lord God" (v. 10).

So the trees of Israel, so lovingly planted one by one, are to be spared, while the weapons of the pillager are used for firewood. It all fits with the frugal, spartan ways of the native Israeli.

It fits, too, with the Israeli tradition of commemorating any struggle for the Holy Land. Following the conflicts in Israel over the establishment of the Israel state, one saw 1948-model trucks and armored weapons—vehicles of every kind—still standing at the sites of their final battles. The Israelies left them by the sides of the roads to remind the people how difficult the land was to attain. A French-built Renault tank stood in the brush at the southern tip of the Sea of Galilee, blasted into submission by a Molotov cocktail. It commemorated the successful defense of unarmed Daganya Kibbutz against a column of twenty-six Syrian tanks in the 1948 war of independence.

It would be fitting indeed for the Israelis to watch a seven-year memorial fire symbolizing still another defense of the Promised Land.

But how can they burn tanks, trucks, and armored vehicles? How can the weapons of modern conflict be destroyed by fire? On this point there is still much controversy. Ezekiel's descriptions are in keeping with his time and his own vocabulary. He speaks of burning "the shields and bucklers, bows and arrows, war clubs and spears" (39:9). His readers and listeners could well understand those terms, though they could not understand the presence of Russia. We can understand the presence of Russia, but have some trouble picturing them invading with archaic weaponry.

Some think Ezekiel's weapons are symbolic representations of the weapons of modern warfare. Perhaps, for example, the reference to the invader coming "like a cloud to cover the land" (38:16) describes air warfare in the language of the sixth century B.C. Bows and arrows might be launchers and rockets. Spears might be rifles.

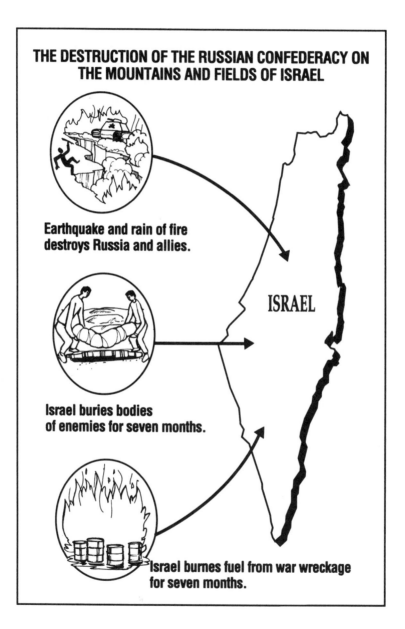

THE DESTRUCTION OF THE RUSSIAN CONFEDERACY ON THE MOUNTAINS AND FIELDS OF ISRAEL

Earthquake and rain of fire
destroys Russia and allies.

ISRAEL

Israel buries bodies
of enemies for seven months.

Israel burnes fuel from war wreckage
for seven months.

But there is another school of thought that takes the prophet absolutely literally Somehow this warfare will revert to use of old-fashioned weapons. We have already seen that the use of horses, though regarded as quite archaic, might be uniquely practical in this particular conflict.

A suggestion has been made many times relating to the oil shortage in the world, and how it might stop all machines someday. Man might revert to more primitive means if his machines fail, but he will never stop his war-making. The soldier with a jammed rifle is glad to have a bayonet and becomes a man with a spear.

This is most speculatory, but here and there are tempting hints of such things. The Russians have perfected an actual wooden rifle. They have compressed wood until it is harder than steel, but lighter to carry. It is still combustible. The Germans used some wooden bullets during World War II; they were cheaper to make and had the desired effect. In fact, they had the virtue of keeping the Allies' doctors overrun with surgery in the fields, since the bullets shattered in flesh and became infectious splinters.

Up-to-date news about poachers shooting bears in the American national parks tells of the use of crossbows instead of rifles. Quieter, cheaper, just as accurate, and just as deadly! It is difficult to imagine a modern nation fielding a land army outfitted with the ancient weapons, however. But, again, it has proved equally difficult to disagree with a biblical prophet.

Another idea is that the fire itself may be unconventional. Ordinarily fire burns wood, but nuclear fire burns metal. God's great fire from heaven that stops the invasion has been considered as a reference to thermonuclear phenomenon. Perhaps the Israelis will have the means to actually burn modern armored weaponry.

Still another speculation on this seven-year fire is acetylene, used in torches that cut, rather than burn, metal. It is still fire, and we do use it to destroy metal, such as in train-wreck rescues.

All these exercises, again, are mere speculation to try to uncover the meanings of Ezekiel's prophecies. But they serve the good purpose of demonstrating that prophecy is not to be summarily discarded because of its archaic language or ancient-seeming settings. Men have learned slowly but surely not to scoff at even the most "dated" terminology of Bible references. As the oft-quoted Ecclesiastes 1:9 puts it, "There is nothing new under the sun."

With the beginning of the seven-year fire, the Russo-Israeli war concludes. There is certainly no doubt of the victor. The aftermath of the war apparently exceeds all post-conflict carnages in man's long history of war. The scavenger beasts and birds are cheated of their foul prey only by full-time burial squads, with the participation of "all the people of the land" and travelers besides. Seven months to bury the dead, seven years to consume the residue of armaments in fire.

What is it all for? For the greater glory of God. Specifically, to testify of the power and the compassion of the Lord, and to explain at last the four-thousand-year tragedy of the chosen people.

For the benefit of the Gentiles, God has shown His glory:

> And I shall set My glory among the nations; and all the nations will see My judgment which I have executed, and My hand which I have laid on them. (Ezekiel 59:21)

For the benefit of the Jews, God has staged this miraculous victory:

And the house of Israel will know that I am the LORD their God from that day onward. (v. 22)

And for the benefit of all, the lesson Ezekiel tried to teach is repeated:

> The house of Israel went into exile for their iniquity because they acted treacherously against Me, and I hid My face from them; so I gave them into the hand of their adversaries, and all of them fell by the sword. (v. 23)

Indeed, all of the prophecies portrayed by Ezekiel's painful demonstrations—the mortification of the prophet before the people's eyes—came to pass just as God originally said they would:

> According to their uncleanness and according to their transgressions I dealt with them, and I hid My face from them. (v.24)

Chapter 39, the conclusion of this great prophecy that began with the dry bones vision and culminated in the Russo-Israeli war, has a happy ending for the Jews. They are to be reconciled to God:

> When I bring them back from the peoples and gather them from the lands of their enemies, then I shall be sanctified through them in the sight of the many nations. Then they will know that I am the LORD their God because I made them go into exile among the nations, and then gathered them again to their own land; and I will leave none of them there any longer. (vv. 27-28)

The section ends with a wonderful promise by God that He will not chastise Israel again and that He has now made the ultimate effort to secure His people.

"And I will not hide My face from them any longer, for I shall have poured out My Spirit on the house of Israel," declares the Lord God. (v. 29)

This final blessing has the characteristic of a messianic deliverance and has caused many interpreters to believe that the battle described earlier is actually the battle of Armageddon. Armageddon immediately precedes the advent of the millennial kingdom, which at last brings real peace.

This is possible, but we think that there are enough distinguishing characteristics between the Russian invasion and the war called Armageddon to consider them to be separate conflicts. We think, however, that the results of the Russian invasion lead directly to Armageddon.

In the next chapter we will discuss this war-to-truly-end-all-wars. No discussion of the affairs of mankind would be complete without Armageddon, the net result of man's efforts without God.

Apparently the demonstration of disaster that is the Russian invasion of Israel is insufficient to impress the world to seek salvation with God. "All the nations will see My judgment which I have executed" (v. 21), says the Lord, but somehow all the heathen get embroiled in Armageddon.

Men will see God in action but will still reject Him. There is nothing new under the sun.

Notes

1. John F. Walvoord, *The Nations in Prophecy* (Grand Rapids: Zondervan. 1967), p. 113.

5

"I Am Against Thee":
Magog in Prophecy

THE USSR THEN AND NOW
THE TWENTIETH AND THE TWENTY-FIRST CENTURIES

From the Bolshevik Revolution to the lowering of the Soviet flag over the Kremlin, Russia has changed. From the inception of Communism in Russia, which made that nation a militant and dangerous force in the world, to the defection and transformation of Shevardnadze and other leading Communists, Russia seemed a constant threat to every nation of the world, not just tiny Israel. But who could have predicted the founding of the new Social Democratic Party in mid-1991, known as we go to press as the Movement of Democratic Reforms? Or who could have predicted the famous three-day coup by the hard-liners, who arrested Mikhail Gorbachev, and the counter-coup by which Russian president Boris Yeltsin freed Gorbachev and initiated the breakup of the Soviet Union into a loose confederacy of republics? Truly, to create some kind of sensible book about contemporary Russia, one has to make a stand in time and review and predict an ongoing series of surprising and sometimes radical changes.

In 1973, the year of publication of the original *The Coming Russian Invasion of Israel*, we stood at a point six years after the Six-Day War in the Middle East and directly in the throes of the Yom Kippur War, the Cold War, Watergate, and Vietnam. Those were complex and challenging times, difficult to explain in a contemporary way and hard to put into the perspective of Ezekiel's prophecy. But though we freely admitted we were somewhat at a loss to explain Ezekiel's scenario in light of the events we saw at that time, there was always a continuing, steady demand for our book among those who had a sincere interest in prophecy. Although a large majority of books published in the seventies went out of print, this one went on through printing after printing, and the interest of the public seemed to show that the message was believable and relevant. Ezekiel, who, as we specified in the original text, was considered simply crazy in his time, was not considered so crazy in the past two decades.

Finally, in 1987, though the basic understanding of the prophetic Scriptures was unchanged and the message of Ezekiel in particular remained just as significant as ever, there were enough changes in world politics that an update of our original text seemed necessary. New personalities had made their entrance on the international stage and new forces were at work to bring about the fulfillment of Ezekiel's visions. The update has also been in steady demand, and it is fair to say that Ezekiel's prophecy is now more widely understood and believed than it was when we issued the original text, especially among evangelical Christians.

Now world events have moved so swiftly and the protagonists of this drama have changed so dramatically that we believe it appropriate to prepare a new book. We hope *Coming: The End!* will bring our readers up-to-date

with the new realities in order to understand more fully
Ezekiel's important revelations.

THE OLD RUSSIA AND EZEKIEL

To review a little of what we said at the beginning of
The Coming Russian Invasion of Israel, the dynamic 38th
and 39th chapters of Ezekiel present the scenario of a
great power to the extreme north of Israel mounting a
massive invasion "in the last days." The great power is
cryptically referred to as "Magog," and it forms a coalition with several other specific nations located in Eastern
Europe, Persia, Ethiopia, and Libya for the purpose of
that attack on Israel. The invading powers will be annihi-
lated—thoroughly destroyed—and Israel will emerge
from the conflict victorious.

The "old Russia" of the seventies and eighties
seemed to fit the scenario perfectly. Here was a vast monolithic superpower to the extreme north of Israel, armed
to the teeth and spiritually, politically, and philosophi-
cally utterly opposed to the fledgling democracy of Israel.
The old Russia constantly supplied arms to the surrounding Arab enemies of Israel and seemed to have the annihilation of that tiny state as a major priority. It would
have been hard to find a better contender for the role of
Magog at that time.

And, in fact, there were several occasions when the
prospect of a Soviet invasion of Israel seemed practically
imminent. In the final stages of the Yom Kippur War in
October 1973, for example, the Soviets actually placed
troops on alert for just such an invasion. At the outset of
the war Israel had been attacked by her Soviet-armed
Arab neighbors on the Day of Atonement, Yom Kippur,
and for once seemed absolutely surprised. Defenses were
down, and Israel seemed to have been lulled into a false
sense of security since her tremendously efficient perfor-
mance in the Six-Day War in 1967. The new attack was to

drag on for several weeks, and the fate of Israel hung in the balance. The Egyptians sent a tank armada so enormous that the largest armored battles in history were waged in the Sinai Desert in that war. It was not at all clear which side would prevail until Israel finally began, in the third week, to push back the mechanized divisions. With steadily increasing force the Israelis managed to drive the army of Egypt across the Suez Canal, and eventually they surrounded several divisions in the desert some distance south of Cairo.

One would think the Western world would have been galvanized by those events, but for all intents and purposes the United States was practically paralyzed, caught up in the political drama of Watergate. The Congress and the press were transfixed by the constitutional crisis caused by the improprieties of President Nixon, and in the midst of all the turmoil, the administration seemed ineffective and preoccupied.

Ultimately, the U.S. government mounted an effort to ship critical military and medical supplies to the beleaguered Jewish nation, but it was constantly hampered. In addition to the internal political paralysis, the United States experienced staunch opposition from the European countries. It seemed that OPEC (Organization of Petroleum Exporting Countries), led by the Arab oil states, had effected a powerful embargo of oil shipments against any nations that helped Israel. By and large, all the European nations (other than Holland) bowed to the Arab pressure and refused to allow the United States landing rights in order to facilitate the shipment of critical supplies to Israel. Only with the greatest difficulty was the American military able to get the shipments to Israel at the same time it was also engaged in the difficult and unpopular war in Vietnam.

In any case, when Israel turned the tide and surrounded the Egyptian army, the Soviet Union became distressed. A military calamity was about to befall its client state, and the Soviet Union put its paratroopers on alert to be sent into the Middle East to save the Egyptians. In response, the United States publicly let it be known that its forces were placed on "red alert" to counter the Soviet threat.

But even as all this intensity heightened and the threat of major superpower war became real indeed, the American press treated the situation as a mere political ploy. Many columnists and the public, too, believed that the dangerous situation actually represented a maneuver by the Nixon administration to divert attention from the significant Watergate events of that precise moment. That was the weekend of the famed "Saturday Night Massacre." Heads rolled as President Nixon, determined to fire his special prosecutor, ended up in opposition to his own government. Absurd as it seems, at a moment when the Soviet Union and Israel, if not the USSR and the United States itself, were on the verge of going to war, the Western world was far more concerned about political events in Washington.

How near to Ezekiel's visions of that final invasion were we in the fall of 1973? Actually, many of Ezekiel's features were in place. The Soviet Union seemed poised to attack, and the United States was thrown into temporary paralysis by its political crisis. Furthermore, many other Arab nations would surely have sided with Egypt and have been supportive of the Soviet Union's efforts to stop Israel. And finally, the monolithic Soviet empire also would have surely been joined by the Warsaw Pact countries of Eastern Europe, which expressed Ezekiel's territories of Gomer and Beth-togarmah (Ezekiel 38:6). So it seemed that much of Ezekiel's scenario was well in place and that the prophecy might be fulfilled at that moment.

But a more exacting examination of the relevant Scriptures shows that some pieces of the puzzle were not quite in place. Persia (principally Iran) was not at that time lined up with the Soviet Union. Indeed, the Shah who then ruled was friendly to the West and conducted equitable trade relations with Israel, shipping oil behind the scenes. Also, Ethiopia, named among Ezekiel's allies of Magog, was cooperative with Israel at that time. It was one of the few places in Africa to which one could directly fly from Israel. In fact, of Ezekiel's Middle Eastern allied aggressors, only Libya was then disposed to work actively with the Soviets against Israel in such a campaign.

So although it might seem, upon casual observation, that many of the pieces were in place, some critical ones were not. And as it happened, the Lord did not accelerate the events to bring about the predicted war. Actually, Israel withdrew its troops from around the Egyptian army, allowing the soldiers to receive supplies from Cairo, the warring nations stepped back from the brink, and the dire moment of near-fulfillment passed.

Still, many people held their breath for some time after the crisis. There was the sense that a Soviet move could occur at any moment. During that time, a few months after the Yom Kippur War, we were involved in producing a film based on the Russian invasion book and with the same title. In the early stages of production the project was almost canceled because the backers were concerned that the Russian invasion of Israel might occur and the film be rendered instantly obsolete through the fulfillment of prophecy. It was necessary to impress upon the investors that there were enough elements missing in the Ezekiel scenario that the fulfillment of the prophecy was evidently not imminent.

Upon publication of *The Coming Russian Invasion of Israel*, we were delighted that Moody Press had such an interest in the subject. We hoped that the entire Chris-

tian world would share that interest. We and the publisher believed that it was important to publish only those
works that were truly worthy of serious consideration by
the reading public.

Initially the publisher expressed some concern about
the identification of Magog with Russia in Ezekiel 38 and
39 and the distinction of the Ezekiel war from Armageddon. But, after some discussion, the questions were
answered and the book was printed.

The book was indeed a success. It has been translated into numerous languages, has been reprinted many
times, has been updated twice, and, during the almost
twenty years since it was first written, has had a steady
reception among those who wish to be informed about
the biblical last days. It is ironic that a book that was com-
paratively difficult to publish has had such longevity.

In some ways, the idea of Russia's invading Israel
has always been in the offing. The Soviets conducted relations with Israel's worst enemies, including Libya and
Marxist Ethiopia, as well as Persia (by arming Iraq, part
of Ezekiel's "Persia"). Also, throughout the 1980s the Soviets conducted relations with the PLO (Palestine Liberation Organization), Israel's prime antagonist. There were
reports of Soviet training of PLO fighters and the storage
of weapons in Lebanon, which caused many to think the
Russian invasion was absolutely imminent. This theory
developed during the "Peace for Galilee" campaign, in
which the Israelis entered Lebanon in 1982 and stayed
for some time, routing Palestinian guerrillas and discov-
ering their caches of arms. Scenarios developed involving the Soviet Union's sending still a new proxy, the
Palestinians, to try to do the job of obliterating Israel.

But still, the Israeli-Lebanese campaign came and
went, Galilee became indeed more secure, and, through it
all, the Soviets did not make their move against Israel. In

point of fact, a startling new development came upon the USSR, one so utterly unpredictable that it stunned the East and West alike: the Soviets suddenly appeared to be the "good guys."

6

Glasnost:
All Quiet on the Eastern Front?

THE END OF THE COLD WAR

The Cold War came to an end so suddenly that the U.S. military, the press, Congress, and the administration all seemed mystified. General Secretary Gorbachev, soon to become President Gorbachev as well, suddenly began to pursue *glasnost*, a new openness, exactly the opposite of past Communist regimes. He also promoted *perestroika*, a relatively free market economic policy seemingly modeled after Western methods and not related to the monolithic Communist style of central control. *Glasnost* and *perestroika* became household words throughout the non-Russian-speaking world. The Berlin Wall came crashing down, and the Warsaw Pact began to dissolve even as we, stunned "victors" of the Cold War, watched. Nuclear treaties were accomplished, and Mikhail Gorbachev became a popular guest of many free world governments. Galvanized by President Gorbachev's personality, President Reagan, Prime Minister Thatcher, and several European heads of state alike praised his vision and forthrightness before the whole world.

Common wisdom indicated that the old animosities were gone and that the former USSR was now a cooperative partner with the free world in establishing a new era of peace. There was much talk about a "peace dividend," a sum of money saved on the Cold War that could now be distributed for domestic purposes in the United States and the other countries that had borne the burden of those hard times. Christian people, students of prophecy, began to wonder if Ezekiel's invasion might be put off to the distant future due to the sudden warming of relations with the nation that appeared to be groomed to play the part of Magog. The Russians were now the good guys.

The television ministry of coauthor Levitt received the following representative letter from the pastor of a large American church:

Dear Zola:

I know that all of us are caught up in the significance of the recent events taking place in Eastern Europe. But the question that is still unclear to me is the prophetic significance of the changes taking place there.

We are aware that the old Roman Empire must be revived, but Bible scholars have generally said that East Germany is Gomer and therefore will side with Russia in the invasion of Israel. In other words, it seems to me that both Daniel's and Ezekiel's prophecies could have been nicely fulfilled even if Eastern Europe had remained Communist and under the control of Russia.

Your insights on this matter are deeply appreciated. I've done some recent studying about prophecy, but I'm simply not clear regarding how today's headlines should be interpreted.

Zola Levitt replied in an editorial in the ministry's newsletter as follows:

Ants on a Painting

We might define some of the pastor's terms. His theology is quite accurate in that Scripture indicates a revival of the former Roman Empire in the same territory
(Western Europe), and it indicates that the area we call
Eastern Europe is where the people called Gomer migrated after the flood. On old biblical maps, Gomer is found
to the northwest of Israel, and modern commentators
have associated it with Eastern Europe. To specify the nation of East Germany as Gomer is a bit too specific, but the
Eastern European area is meant. Some teachers refer to it
as the "Danube territories."

The prophets specified, respectively, that the Empire would be revived (Daniel 7:19-28) and that the disposition of Gomer toward Israel would be hostile (Ezekiel
38:5-6).

And truly the prophecy would be clearly understood
if everything had stayed the way it was last winter—that is,
if the old rules of Communism had remained and Eastern
Europe was still, in effect, a Russian satellite and ally. People are now asking what happened to the prophecy of the
coming Russian invasion of Israel and the participation of
Eastern Europe, just as this letter indicates.

(Well, first of all, we ought to understand that all
prophecy will happen as written, whether or not we understand it or are skillful in applying it to what we observe of the world situation.)When Tom McCall and I first
published our book on this subject, *The Coming Russian
Invasion of Israel*, Moody Press, the publisher was skeptical of the theory. Was Russia really going to invade Israel,
the editor in chief asked, and should we just state it that
way in black and white? Once we explained our analysis
of Ezekiel's invasion of Gog and Magog (Ezekiel 38-39),
that careful and conservative publisher accepted the
book. It was an immediate best-seller then and still is
now. What makes the book fascinating are the things seen
by Ezekiel, not the observations of us modern writers. In

every age Christians attempt to fit the prophecies into their own worldly situations, and that is probably a worthy thing to do. We are not to be asleep as the children of darkness (1 Thessalonians 5:3-6); we are to observe the world around us and draw conclusions. We can draw wrong ones and we can miss subtleties in the prophecies, but we are to be thinking about those things and not ignoring them, as are the nonbiblically studied people around us.

In its time, World War I looked just like Armageddon. World War II and Hitler looked to many believers like the Tribulation Period and the Antichrist. In both cases, important pieces of the prophecies were missing in the worldly events. Israel, for example, was not back in its land until after the Second World War, so key Tribulation prophecies such as the rebuilding of the Temple could not reasonably be foreseen. Bible readers adjusted their scholarship accordingly, but did not drop the idea of watching for the prophecies to be fulfilled. In like manner, the former configuration of the states of Eastern Europe looked very good in light of the pictures of Daniel and Ezekiel of the end times, but other configurations may work as well in these prophecies. We must finally remember that all will be fulfilled because, as the Lord put it, "It is written."

The tendency of Bible readers to want to place prophecy fulfillment in their own times has been at work here with the prophecy of the Russian invasion of Israel. Teachers have taught throughout this generation, and I am certainly one of them, that the prophecy seems imminent, and it still does, in my view. But, biblically speaking, we have only the evidence that this prophecy will be fulfilled between the restoration of the Jewish people back to their land, Israel, and the inception of the Kingdom to come, when the sanctuary will be rebuilt in Jerusalem (see Ezekiel's "dry bones" vision in chap. 37). We have seen, and are still seeing, the restoration of the Jews back to the Land. This is an ongoing process that began in earnest in 1948 and is receiving an enormous impetus now, with the Jews coming out of Russia bound for Israel.

The tension between the formerly communistic Russian Empire and Israel was obvious until last winter, but anti-Semitism persists and in some ways is even greater in the Soviet Union of today. An increase in freedom means an increase in both positive and negative elements in a society. The Russian anti-Semites, called *Pamyat*, are every bit as vicious as were the Nazis of the thirties, and, if they had their way, Israel would be torched tomorrow. The same elements persist throughout Eastern Europe.

The problem with trying to fit a prophecy fulfillment into the huge picture of ongoing contemporary events is that we have little perspective as individual human beings of the tapestry of global affairs. Imagine tiny ants walking on a gigantic painting, each one trying to judge what is depicted. Add to that the fact that we seem to be in an uncomfortable period of transition in certain crucial parts of the world, most notably the Soviet Union and Eastern Europe, and it is difficult to anchor our wishful prophecy thinking on solid ground.

But a few things are clear even in this transitory time. First, the road to democracy is overwhelmingly strewn with obstacles. We can see troubles even now in Romania, which last December was a most refreshing example of a land in which freedom seemed to spring forth from the very stones. Now the Romanians are picketing again and lambasting the new government as being too much like the old one. The entire Soviet Union itself is having enormous troubles, which I do not have to list here. When Zbigniew Brezinski was the guest of Ted Koppel on "Nightline" recently, he pictured three different futures for the U.S.S.R. and sadly stated that all of them involved major violence. If the U.S.S.R. is headed for democracy, he reasoned, there will be much resistance and many calamities over that. If, on the other hand, it splits off into nationalist regimes, as the Baltic governments are now trying to do, then there will be much rivalry and still more trouble. And finally, if there is reaction against the present *perestroika* and a form of Communism returns, then there will be much rebellion against restoration of the old order.

It is in the third theory, the reactionary force theory, that one could see a spiteful Russian invasion of a small country like Israel as logical in the Russian mind. I have previously said in these pages that a foreign adventure could be a communist way of galvanizing the Soviet people under one flag again. And, of course, the takeover of Israel would be a very profitable adventure, if only they could get the job done.

We might also look to a whole new view of what an invasion amounts to in the modern world. Until recently, whole nations attacked other whole nations, but the newest look in warfare has to do with small but extremely deadly forces with devastating weaponry out of all proportion to their numbers. In other words, a small force of Russian and East European reactionaries could well join with terroristic forces already well established in Persia, Ethiopia, and Libya to launch a potentially lethal invasion of Israel. With weapons such as nuclear ballistics and poison gas, one could see how a relatively few people, not necessarily authorized under the central governments of their nations, could effect a deathblow on a tiny nation like Israel. In fact, in the past, commentators have wondered why the Soviet Union, with all its might, fully one hundred times the size of Israel in population, would need many allies to carry out such an invasion. Perhaps the small force theory better fits the times.

All of the above is only an exercise in speculation, of course. I am one of those ants on the painting, and I do not know what the whole picture is about either. But I can say this: Ezekiel's prophecy still looks imminent, and the configuration of nations that he selected in his foresight is still perfectly reasonable for that deadly undertaking. I have never been convinced that the Soviet Union and Eastern Europe are less dangerous now than they were before. As a matter of fact, the desperation of their economic circumstances might make them behave very foolishly at some future point.

Shortly after the "Ants on a Painting" appeared, some significant negatives began to appear in connection with *glasnost* and *perestroika*. The world began to see the apparent dismantling of the Soviet empire. Lithuania and the other Baltic republics initiated their own declarations of independence from the central Soviet government. In addition, several interior provinces developed independence movements of their own. The central government dealt with each case individually, trying to solve some problems with the tongue and others with the teeth. Violence developed in certain provinces and gunfire was heard in the streets of places that had been silent on matters of politics since the Bolshevik Revolution. There was genuine concern about some kind of civil war in the huge and far-flung Soviet Union.

Western analysts began to understand that the public face of the USSR was far different from what was actually happening behind the scenes. Reports stressed that the Soviet army was still huge, very much intact, and invariably under the control of the central government— still very much Communistic. Furthermore, the apparatus of the dreaded KGB, the secret police force, was still in place and in control of the politics of the faltering central government. The "uncommon" wisdom suggested that the apparently cooperative attitude of the Soviet Union had been merely a ruse all along to allow the Soviets to redeploy its considerable forces.

The nervous period from the destruction of the Berlin Wall to the beginning of the Persian Gulf War was characterized by helter-skelter developments of all sorts throughout the Soviet Union and Eastern Europe. The East Germans were broke and discouraged. The Romanians could not get comfortable with their new government. Yugoslavia came apart at the seams. Body counts rose in the Baltics, and Poland suffered under a sudden transition to a free market, with its considerable pressure and forces. And the huge Soviet Union reeled as independent elections in the provinces gave birth to new ideas and even new political parties.

RETURN OF THE "EVIL EMPIRE"

Some began to think that the original USSR of the brutal times of Brezhnev and Stalin was returning. Ronald Reagan's "Evil Empire" was back, and the new experiment had not only faltered but really failed. It seemed that Gorbachev had created a monster. The separate republics were bolting, and separatism became the new look in the USSR. As the world watched to see how Moscow would respond to the various secession movements, the old familiar face of totalitarian Communism was evident as Gorbachev ordered or allowed his army forces to repress the democratic movements in Lithuania and other republics. Once again the Red Army was ascendant in Soviet politics, and the shadowy KGB reared its ugly serpentine head as the true power behind the throne. Somehow it all seemed as though *glasnost* had shifted into reverse.

For a few days in August 1991, in fact, the hard-liners actually were in control. They declared a national emergency, put Gorbachev under house arrest, and tried to put the Soviet Union back on the old track of centralized Communism. But Boris Yeltsin and his Russian Republic parliament held firm, resisted the army tanks, and, with Western power encouragement, ousted the ousters. To the amazement of the world, Gorbachev and Yeltsin, old rivals, for a while cooperated in restructuring the country into what has been called the Soviet Dis-union.

Most recently, the Soviet Union has been completely dissolved, and Russia, itself, has become the dominant republic. It seems very pertinent that when Ezekiel described the future antagonist of Israel he used the term "Prince of Rosh." It should come as no surprise to anyone who believes the Bible that Russia is emerging as the primary force out of the ashes of the Soviet Union.

Obviously it is difficult in a book with a given publication date to keep up with rapid geopolitical developments. By the time this manuscript is read, all sorts of events may have transpired inside and outside of the former Soviet Union, which may have a significant bearing on its internal structure and its international aspirations. Suffice it to say here, however, that the potential threat of Russia with regard to the Middle East in general and Israel in particular is in no way a thing of the past. Russia is still very much capable of undertaking the invasion prophesied by Ezekiel and, in some ways, that event seems all the more likely in these uncertain times. All things considered, the old Communistic USSR seemed more comfortable and predictable than the new fractionalized and struggling republics.

On a related development, the ominous rise of anti-Semitism in Russia is noteworthy. For centuries anti-Jewish attitudes have been strong among the Russians, and many pogroms and persecutions have taken place. Jewish people descended from those trapped in Russia are almost uniform in their condemnation of Russian intolerance toward the Jewish people, and now, just as the official control of Communism appears to recede, the ugly aspects of ancient hatreds come to the fore. As we mentioned earlier, the movement is organized enough to have a name, *Pamyat*, which means memory (as though there were something awful to remember about the Jewish people in Russia). It was as though anti-Semitism had been frozen under the ice of totalitarian Communism and the thaw has brought it back to life.

Antagonism against the Jews in Russia will give added impetus to the already strong movement among Soviet Jews to get out of the country in a massive exodus to Israel. Millions of Jewish people have been waiting for countless years for the opportunity to simply leave, but until recently there was only a trickle as the "refuseniks" have grudgingly been permitted to emigrate to the West, in general, and Israel, in particular. But the floodgates are beginning to open, and some 3 million Jews who remained in the former Soviet Union are beginning to stream out to Israel. When they all come, they will nearly double the Jewish population in the already strained and beleaguered Jewish state, but they will be welcomed with open arms, as have Jews from virtually every nation of the world.

Obviously, anti-Semitic Russian attitudes will help foment the invasion. Whatever reason is given for this superpower's invading little Israel, anti-Semitism will facilitate it. And historically there has been no shortage of that among the Russian people.

7

The New Alliances:
The New World Order

THE PERSIAN GULF WAR

The Persian Gulf War was utterly unpredictable. Even in this end-times world, with its many false prophets and with the production of horoscopes and the like at an all-time high, it seems that no one could have forecast the mind of Saddam Hussein. Even after that tyrant invaded Kuwait, it was still hard to foresee that the United States and some twenty-eight other nations would have more than .5 million military personnel fighting a war during the winter of 1991. Truly, world politics can shift and bring about new alliances almost instantly.

Prior to August 2, 1990, the day of the surprise attack on Kuwait, Iraq was a somewhat dubious friend of the Western powers, acting as a counterweight to the unpredictable government of Iran. For eight long years the two Muslim neighbors had been deadlocked in a ferocious war that was extremely costly in terms of casualties and matériel. Saddam Hussein had indeed played the East against the West and had enjoyed the constant support of the Soviet Union for his arms. Even as the war was winding down in a cease-fire there were ominous news stories about Iraq's attempting to fabricate an enormous supergun capable of shooting explosive devices, perhaps even nuclear devices, over hundreds of miles.

Not yet cured of constant warfare and its heavy cost, Iraq began threatening its tiny but oil-rich neighbor Kuwait. Those threats had been heard for some time, but this time massive troop movements were evident as the Iraqi army piled up along the Kuwaiti border. There were many tense days of comings and goings in the Middle East as Saudi Arabia, Egypt, Jordan, and other Arab nations attempted to dissuade Hussein from his apparent plan to invade Kuwait. From their point of view, war with Iran was more excusable in that the Iranians, though certainly Muslims, are not Arabs; it was quite another matter in their view to fight another Arab nation such as Kuwait.

Diplomatic pressure mounted as Europe and the United States began to urge against Iraq's military action and the dictator Hussein appeared to be listening. But, in the end, all of that failed, and on that fateful day in August an awesome army of hundreds of thousands of Iraqi soldiers, along with planes, helicopters, and tanks, rapidly overwhelmed their nearly defenseless neighbor and subjugated the nation of Kuwait.

It was not an unheard-of event in twentieth-century politics. The world had seen numerous such invasions of one country by another, especially in Asia and Africa. At times the nations of the world have practically ignored such incursions as mere regional concerns. At other times, such as in the two world wars, the world community has considered its vital interests to be at stake and intervened to protect those interests. This time the Iraqi invasion was not considered a mere regional dispute; it seemed instead to be an event of world-shaking importance due to the existence of the massive oil reserves under the desert sands of Kuwait.

News reports stated that Iraq possessed about 10 percent of the world's known oil reserves, and Kuwait had an additional 15 percent. With Saddam Hussein occupying Kuwait, one lunatic dictator controlled one-fourth of the oil of the whole world. Furthermore, the Iraqi army, hardly exercised by its easy conquest, was now positioning itself along the border between Kuwait and Saudi Arabia. Within a few hundred miles an additional 25 percent of the world's known oil reserves were defended by a Saudi army that was not much better prepared than the hapless Kuwaitis.

With another lightning attack, the Iraqi military could move its considerable forces south and west and, in perhaps a week, have under its control about one-half of the known oil on the planet. Obviously that was not a petty matter. The attention of the whole earth shifted to the Middle East as never before. Only two times in history have the nations of the world seemed so deeply concerned with Middle Eastern matters—during the Roman war against Israel in the first century and the European war of the Crusades against the Muslim rulers of the Holy Land in the tenth and eleventh centuries.

The idea of a maverick dictatorship such as Iraq controlling huge oil reserves was an intolerable prospect for the nations of the world. Even the several stunning Arab-Israeli wars during the past several decades did not capture the attention of the nations as did the swift action by the "Butcher of Baghdad." The "kings of the earth" could easily picture their economies and, indeed, their very survival threatened by small, primitive Iraq, heretofore a country of little consequence.

In rare concord the nations were galvanized into action, with the United Nations serving as their forum. The Kuwaiti government in exile asked for help in restoring its conquered country, and Saudi Arabia asked for aid in defending itself and its oil wells against what appeared to be an impending invasion by Iraq. The United States took the lead in responding to the invasion of Kuwait, and President Bush called for the United Nations to formulate resolutions against Iraq. Actions taken to repulse the invasion would be perfectly legal, approved by a majority of nations of the world. The United States placed shock troops at the front on the Kuwaiti border and undertook a grand buildup of tremendous forces in Saudi Arabia. Diplomatic pressure also built up as the UN passed stronger and stronger resolutions, and many other smaller forces joined the United States in a coalition against Iraq. In the end, half a million troops backed by a dozen UN resolutions and some twenty-eight sovereign nations were gathered against the aggressor, with even the Soviet Union acquiescing to the will of the UN against its client state, Iraq.

But Saddam Hussein refused to budge. He would not give up Kuwait. He felt he could rally the masses of the Arabs to him against the foreign "invaders" and against the sheikhs who ruled various Arab nations. It seemed that he thought that even if he lost this early round he could survive as an Arab hero in the convoluted politics of the Middle East. He perceived himself a modern representation of the famous Saladin, who led the Muslims of the eleventh century against the European Crusaders and rid the Arab world of the detested foreign presence. In another role, Hussein considered himself to be a new Nebuchadnezzar, king of ancient Babylon, resurrecting the power and glory of that primeval empire over the entire region. He called Kuwait his "nineteenth province," and he threatened to destroy all of Iraq's enemies, especially Israel, if anyone tried to force his hand. And thus the stage was set for the war.

The first "television war" began at prime time following the evening news in the United States when most everyone was at home and comfortably able to gather around their TV sets. As the air attacks began on Baghdad and the spectacular fireworks of the antiaircraft tracer rounds arched into the skies above the distant capital, we watched transfixed, so close and yet so far. We were horrified as Scud missiles were lofted against Saudi Arabia—one of the combatants—and even Israel, a non-combatant nation quietly sitting by in an unaccustomed role as an observer of a Middle Eastern war. The attack on Israel gave an eerie prediction of things to come. The amount of hatred shown by the Jordanians and by Palestinians within Israel—they actually danced in the streets to celebrate missiles falling on civilian Tel Aviv—gave some prediction of the strength of the Arab motivation for the coming Russian invasion of Israel.

It was an almost surreal experience to watch live action from ten thousand miles away as reporters whom we had come to know by face and name were suddenly interrupted by sirens and had to stop their work and don gas masks. We were proud of our troops, our news coverage, and our Patriot missiles, which in many cases downed the incoming Scuds. Finally, after air superiority had been achieved and various Iraqi military installations and supply lines had been pounded many times over, the ground war began—and ended quickly. "The mother of all surrenders" began almost immediately as the exhausted Iraqis—touted as the fourth largest army in the world—suddenly became, as one soldier put it, "the second largest army in Iraq."

The United States called it a day, and Saddam Hussein remains, at press time, in power in Iraq, still causing considerable agony in that part of the world. For one thing, he seems to be continuing to build nuclear weapons, despite UN sanctions to the contrary, and he has thwarted inspections of his installations. Iraq's willingness to continue to arm in the face of all it has gone through and in opposition to the vast majority of the nations of the world is strikingly suggestive of the strange times in which we live.

Almost everything about this war and its aftermath has been unpredictable. Most of the Arab nations, for example, had long been at each others' throats but reluctantly agreed to band together with non-Muslim foreigners to thwart the aggression of Iraq. Even Syria, so active in anti-Western terrorism, cooperated with the Allies in this effort. Iran played a strange role of its own. After its bloody eight-year war against Iraq, one would have supposed Iran would have lined up against its enemy, but evidently Persian Iran hated the Western influence in the Muslim Middle East even more than it hated Iraq. Unhappy to see an array of foreigners threaten the soil of the revered Muslim sacred cities of Mecca and Medina, Iran became neutral in this war and actually something of a beneficiary to Iraq in that it accepted the remaining Iraqi air force, which limped over the border to Iran for sanctuary during the bombing.

So at press time we have quite a puzzling world in the aftermath of the Persian Gulf War. How does this world relate to the kind of world described by the prophet Ezekiel in the end times? Is it still conceivable that a powerful nation to the extreme north of Israel will someday invade the Holy Land along with a number of allies and be cataclysmically destroyed in the process?

THE NEW RUSSIA

We explained in the original text of this book, *The Coming Russian Invasion of Israel*, that Magog in prophecy represents the modern Russian area, but we do have a different Russia now than we had in the seventies. Instead of the old monolithic Communist power of the Cold War, the former Soviet Union now appears to be a divided and collapsing empire, economically, politically, and militarily. The old USSR seems drastically weakened and hardly a major factor in world affairs anymore.

But is it really weak? How strong is the Russian army? How powerful is the KGB, the secret police system? Are the army and the KGB perhaps waiting in the wings to take over if chaos develops? And even if the old Soviet Union is transformed into something far different, would it still be willing and able to launch an invasion of Israel? Most of the population and resources of the former Soviet Union are in the province of Russia itself. It is by far the largest among all the republics of the old USSR, and it remains extremely well armed. Would Russia alone be capable of bringing about the invasion described in Ezekiel?

Some think that an invasion of a different sort, a small but devastating terroristic event, could answer Ezekiel's prophecy and that the reactionary Communist forces might well be capable of pulling it off. That is to say, within the large, disorganized group of previous Soviet republics there is still an element capable of such an invasion and capable of allying with similar elements in Eastern Europe and the Middle East to make it happen. All we know for certain is that the prophecy uttered by the Lord's prophet will come to pass. Timing is not specified except as "in the last days." Whether that nation to the extreme north known as Magog is Russia as we know it today or is some other future form of that country is not apparent from the prophecy. Nevertheless, some form of government from those people to Israel's extreme north will organize with the "evil thought" to invade Israel. That situation may well be taking shape in what we are seeing today.

PERSIA AND BABYLON

While Russia wrestles with its domestic troubles, Iran and Iraq have suddenly become major players on the world stage. Even though Iraq has been devastated by the Gulf War, it has remained intact and, at this time, is still capable of causing considerable difficulties. Iraq has frankly admitted that it is preparing nuclear weapons (after lying about it previously and trying to subvert UN inspections of its nuclear facilities). Saddam Hussein has solemnly promised to "annihilate half of Israel" and seems to be working hard to perfect the means to do so.

Modern Iraq and Iran are part of the old Babylonian and Persian empires. Both Persia and Babylon are mentioned extensively in the end times scenarios of the biblical prophets. Persia, Ezekiel pointed out, is one of the primary allies of Magog in the future war against Israel. It is interesting that one of the main beneficiaries of the Gulf War was Iran, the heart of ancient Persia. Out of the conflict it gained what appears to be a permanent cease-fire with Iraq, a certain portion of land it had lost to Iraq during the eight-year war they had with each other, and a fairly modern air force from the dozens of war planes that retreated to Iran from Iraq for refuge.

"Persia" seems to be taking her place for the drama of the coming Russian invasion of Israel. We will discuss the future of Babylon in a later chapter.

ETHIOPIA AND "OPERATION SOLOMON" (OR THE PUSH FROM CUSH)

Ethiopia has never been considered a major force, and in the past it was difficult to see why Ezekiel would name it as a primary ally of Magog in the invasion. But that nation is changing rapidly as we go to press. With the withdrawal of Soviet support for the dictatorship of Mengistu, that dictator has fled, and the government is at this writing in the hands of Marxist rebels. Unfortunately, both sides in the Ethiopian civil war of so many years were Marxists with allegiance to Moscow, and thus the enmity toward Israel goes on.

At this moment Ethiopia is receiving some aid and is in less dire circumstances than in the past. As a strengthened but still Marxist force to the south of Israel, it will be a factor of some importance in the upcoming invasion.

In the original text of Ezekiel, the prophet uses the term Cush, which is translated "Ethiopia" and certainly involves the area of the current nation of that name. But some believe that Cush may well have also included much of Africa along with present day Ethiopia. Thus, if more of the African nations are involved, it is easier to see how much of a force that distracting southern attack would be to Israel.

Two stories have emerged recently from Ethiopia that poignantly depict the awful circumstances of that strife-ridden African nation. One concerns the remarkable exodus of thousands of Ethiopian Jews, known as Falashas, to Israel. In the midst of civil war and terrible famine those hapless people appealed to be taken to what they claim as their ancient homeland, and arrangements were made behind the scenes between Israel, the Ethiopian government (which demanded arms and aid in return for the Falashas), and neutral airlines. At first, the remarkable and very humanitarian action was done in secret, but finally the news media discovered what amounted to a true human interest story of kindness and generosity in an increasing cold and brutal area of the world. They televised the black Jewish people, most of whom had never been on an airplane before, being packed into jumbo jets and flown to the Promised Land.

The massive exodus was termed "Operation Solomon" by the Israeli government. The use of Solomon's name was germane to the Falashas' claim to be Jews. They have carried on the traditions of Judaism from ancient times because, they say, they are descendants of

King Solomon and the Queen of Sheba. (Scripture does not confirm any marriage or personal relationship between Solomon and the queen, and certainly not any children, but the strict law-keeping and sincere Jewish traditional practices of the Falashas go back very far and are most impressive to see. They believe strongly in their descendancy, and they practice what they preach. The religious authorities of Israel were most impressed with their faith, and they seem to have become a beneficial element in Israeli society almost immediately. People who were starving on the dry and empty sands of Ethiopia have become useful citizens in a twentieth-century democracy almost overnight. And the world has watched in wonder at this first example of black Africans being taken somewhere literally for their own good and not for the profit of those who transported them.

The other story is also related to the famine that has ravaged Ethiopia. It seems that the American soldiers who still remain in the Middle East in the aftermath of Desert Storm have grown increasingly unhappy with their field rations, known today as MREs, or "Meals Ready to Eat," in military parlance. Descended from the notorious C Rations of earlier wars, the MREs are disdained by young Americans used to a much more luxurious diet. The dried and reconstituted meals were consequently nicknamed by the troops "Meals Rejected by Ethiopians." But the joke has come close to reality since the Defense Department has canceled all future orders of MREs, and the millions of units now in stock will be sent to the starving people of Ethiopia. The story is a sad commentary on the plight of those trapped on a battlefield of infertile soil for so very long.

If the new government of Ethiopia succeeds in ending the civil unrest of the country, that may in the end simply make that nation a more effective ally of the Soviets in the upcoming invasion, and actually the strengthening of Ethiopia since we wrote the original text of this book better qualifies it for its role in the prophecy. If a larger land area is meant, then the attention of Israel's defense forces will be that much more diverted by an attack on its weakest border, the southern Negev Desert, which contains the town of Dimona, the center of Israel's nuclear weaponry.

LIBYA

At the time of the publication of the original book it was a bit difficult to see Libya's role, as well. The problem was the same as with Ethiopia; the country was in such bad shape and was so minor a power that it was unclear just how much it could be of help to the invading Magog. But Libya has really come of age as an enemy of Israel—and of much the rest of the world as well. During most of the eighties that nation, under Moammar Qaddafi, was a dominant force in the murky world of terrorism. A Bedouin strongman, often preferring to be filmed in a desert tent, Qaddafi postured repeatedly on television as a leader who could call to action minions of terror at will to strike at an airline here or a political figure there. Libyan terrorists were willing to kidnap, maim, or kill hostages throughout Europe and around the world. And there were two air battles in which Libyan fighter pilots engaged the U.S. Navy, to Libya's regret.

But Libya has been quieter since the nighttime raid of bombers from the United States. Either they have backed off from their schemes to a large extent, or they have gone so far underground that no terrorist claims to work for Libya anymore. Nevertheless, that nation continues to pursue chemical weaponry, aided by European companies who have been convicted of supplying poison gas to various radical Middle Eastern powers (including Iraq). There can be little doubt that, given the opportunity, Libya would rush to join Russia and the other northern powers, and Persia and Ethiopia, in the invasion styled by Ezekiel.

Clearly Libya and the other nations we have reviewed are in a far better posture now to conduct this aggression than they were in the seventies or eighties. Although the old USSR appeared much stronger on the surface and a more likely invader of Israel, its allies were not nearly so ready to give assistance. And these days allies or coalitions of nations have become very important in warfare. The USSR would have looked extremely brutal in a unilateral attack against Israel, but if Russia could appear to be just one of a group of nations, all with some seemingly legitimate grudge against that small power, the invasion would look more reasonable in the eyes of the world.

8

The Gulf War Precedent: One of Many Threats to Israel

THE PERSIAN GULF PRECEDENT

With the Persian Gulf War, the United States created what President Bush calls a "New World Order," in which significant disputes could be taken to the Security Council of the United Nations. In a new atmosphere of cooperation between the United States and the Soviet Union, resolutions could be passed against aggressor nations anywhere, and they would have force. The deadlock of détente being long gone, the superpowers voted together against Iraq. Resolutions passed by the UN through the winter of 1990-91 had teeth, as numerous nations sent representative forces and funds to back up the massive buildup of primarily American forces in the Persian Gulf. Thus it was shown that if a nation wantonly commits aggression against its neighbor, the aggressor can expect almost universal condemnation and perhaps even military confrontation. At least that is the theory.

One cannot help wondering if the remarkable new tool of international peacekeeping might not someday be utilized against American interests and, most particularly, against the state of Israel. It seems that the Gulf War set a precedent in international relations that could be dangerous to the Promised Land. From the point of view of most of the member countries of the United Nations, Israel is an aggressor state. Though the condemnations of the UN have poured down for decades on that tiny country for almost everything it has done, the new situation is grave. These are not the days when Israel is condemned for defending itself against terrorism or for doing archeological digs at the ancient Temple Mount in Jerusalem; the heart of the new criticism is that the UN, by and large, considers Israel's capture of the land from Jerusalem eastward to the Jordan River during the Six-Day War in 1967 an act of aggression. In the eyes of the UN, Israel is now in the position of an occupying military power. The land in question, of course, is the West Bank, and the Arab populations living in the occupied area have come to call themselves Palestinians.

The Palestinians claim to have an indigenous local culture, and they insist that they have historically lived in the land. They believe that the Jewish people have no right at all to the land and that it was always their own. From the Israeli point of view, the land was given to the Jewish people by God; no one else can lay any claim to it, however long they may have occupied it while the rightful owners were away. Both ideas—that the Palestinians have a culture of their own in that land and that the Jews have no claim to it—are certainly open to question. But for our purposes now we wish to call attention only to what is called Israel's occupation of the West Bank. We will discuss the Palestinian question in more detail later.

Israel, of course, is a member of the United Nations and gives its point of view often. It was the Jews who were attacked by their surrounding Arab neighbors—neighbors who loudly and publicly threatened to push the Israelis into the Mediterranean Sea. That threat was widely published.) Remarkably, /Israel has withstood allied Arab attacks over and over again, seemingly leading to the situation where an even stronger alliance would be needed to accomplish the so-called liberation of the supposedly occupied territories.) The Israelis responded to the threat of extinction by capturing their ancient homeland areas, which they call Judaea and Samaria, creating a buffer zone between them and their enemies. The strip of land in question ranges from about fifteen to thirty miles in width and separates Israel, primarily established on the Mediterranean coast, from the inland Arab states of Jordan, Iraq, Iran, and the smaller Gulf states. The Golan Heights help insulate Israel from Syria, and the Gaza Strip lies between Israel and Egypt (though Egypt has been no problem since it made peace with Israel in the Camp David Accords). The Israelis unquestionably think that they need the territories in dispute in order to protect themselves against further incursions, and they are, in fact, settling them slowly with immigrants from the Soviet Union and around the world.

Part and parcel with that new program of occupation and resettlement of the territories was the capture of Jerusalem. Israel annexed it and made it the capital of the country, as it was in King David's time. The latter action has not been recognized as legal by any major power, and not one has moved its embassy from the old capital of Tel Aviv to Jerusalem.

The UN has collectively and repeatedly rejected Israel's arguments for security and considers Israel an aggressor against its neighbors, an occupier of foreign lands, and an oppressor of those who live in those lands.) Indeed, the majority view of Israel worldwide is not substantially different from the world's view of Iraq when it conquered and occupied Kuwait. It should be remembered, however, that the response by the United States and almost every other nation was overwhelmingly powerful against Iraq and, in the chronology of geopolitical actions, quite swift.

It is not beyond imagination that the UN could decide that similar action is required against Israel. Thus far, the lone veto of the United States in the Security Council has protected Israel from more condemnation than it has already sustained, and perhaps even more militant action. But what if pressure mounted concerning Israel's withdrawal from the West Bank and the "internationalization" of Jerusalem? Would economic sanctions be applied and then, perhaps, military confrontation, as with Iraq? What if the United States believed it could no longer protect Israel with its veto? What if the Soviet Union, Iran, Iraq, and the Arab and African nations together pressed for resolutions forcing Israel to withdraw or else? It would appear that a dangerous precedent has been set for the solution of such problems. In the eyes of most of the nations of the world, the USSR and a coalition of allies attacking little Israel for its occupation of Palestinian territories would not be substantially different from the United States and its coalition attacking Iraq for its occupation of Kuwait.

If Israel remained intransigent against such pressure, one could well imagine the concerned nations telling the United States to "stay out of this one," much as the Soviet Union passively sat out the Gulf War. Europe might also sit on the sidelines in such a conflict and observe while the nations actively opposed to Israel settle the matter of its so-called aggression. It is not difficult to imagine such a scenario given today's reality and the precedents already set at the United Nations in what is called the New World Order. Could it be through just such a scenario as we have before us today that Ezekiel's prophecy of a massive attack against Israel will be accomplished?

THE WARM WATER PORTS THEORY REVISITED

The Russian bear is hardly toothless or fully tamed at this point. The army and the KGB are much in evidence and the struggling central government made some frightening moves against its own occupied territories, as in the Baltics. Although Leningrad may be going back to its old historical name of St. Petersburg, and though the shackles of socialism appear to be falling off all over Eastern Europe and the former Soviet Union, it should be remembered that Russia was an occupying power long before it went Communistic. It was the dream of the czars to occupy and control the land from the Atlantic and Mediterranean in the West to the Pacific in the East. And the theories of Lenin, Stalin, and company made significant inroads in that ambitious project. But a constantly irritating obstacle to that dream of centuries has been Russia's lack of control over warm water ports. Russia's mainland ports are iced over during the winter, and its prodigious navy is handicapped by that incontrovertible fact. Americans don't often consider that we live in a land with year-round accessible ports on three sides of our country, but that has been a serious and almost humiliating problem for the northern lands of the USSR.

Obviously, secure access to the Mediterranean would be a logical Russian goal. It always was, and it certainly still is. The Middle East was always intriguing to the Soviet Union for that reason, in addition to its vast oil reserves. The fact is, even if the world were to find some substitute energy source so that oil was no longer a major issue, Russia would still be powerfully attracted to the Mediterranean ports of the Middle East, and Israel in particular, as the gateway to Africa.

THE "PALESTINIAN PROBLEM"

As we observed in the section about UN precedents, the Palestinian problem may be germane to the fulfillment of the prophecy. Israel insists on the lands of Judaea and Samaria for a defense buffer and for settlement of millions of immigrants yet to come from the former Soviet Union and elsewhere, whereas the Arabs claim that the West Bank is historically their land, taken forcibly from them by Israel. Crucial also in the dispute is the fate of Jerusalem, the location of the primary holy sites of Islam and Christianity as well as Judaism. The Muslims, for their part, obviously want to regain control of the city, and the official position of the Roman Catholic Pope is that Jerusalem should be "internationalized." In the face of all that, the Jewish people want the city to remain in their hands as their central religious shrine and the political capital of their nation.

The latest and most attention-getting strategy adopted by the Palestinians is the *intifada*, a semiviolent method of protest by which the Arabs in the West Bank have demonstrated their dissatisfaction with the situation. There have been strikes, work stoppages, riots, various terror activities, stabbings and bombings against Israeli civilians, and attacks with rocks on the armed troops who come to try to control the disruptions. Much of the world has rallied to the cause of the Palestinians, but still Israel believes it has no place to retreat. The Israeli government is resolute in holding onto the land, describing any other solution to Israel's defense as "suicide."

For Bible believers, one of the most interesting disruptions occurred during the time of the winter buildup of Desert Shield against Iraq. It all started when a small but determined group in Jerusalem decided it would stage a peaceful demonstration at the Western Wall urging the rebuilding of the Temple on the Temple Mount.

The Temple will indeed be rebuilt in the end times on Mount Moriah in Jerusalem, where it was before. That is one of the key elements in the end-times scenario, along with the Antichrist and the second coming of Christ Himself. But in the current situation the Israelis, by and large, have neither the religious inclination nor the political stomach to rebuild the Temple. Most of them, truth to tell, do not think that the Temple, with its priesthood and sacrifices, is necessary or desirable to modern Jewish faith. And furthermore, they do not want to antagonize the Muslims further by appearing to threaten their holy site, the Shrine of the Dome of the Rock, which now stands on the Temple Mount. That third most sacred site of Islam, a gold-colored dome and a magnificent mosaic building, has sat atop the Temple Mount for 1,300 years, and undoubtedly the Muslims would not tolerate its disturbance by the Israelis, particularly so that the Jews could rebuild their own Temple on that site.

But, say some religious Jews, the Temple of God was on that site previously during the time of Solomon and again during the Second Temple period, leading to the entrance of Jesus on the world scene, until the Romans destroyed it in A.D. 70. The little group in Jerusalem has a certain amount of support and is determined to demonstrate in favor of the new Temple. Interestingly enough, it was the Israeli court system itself that blocked the group's demonstration, and the matter went on to the Supreme Court of the country. The jurists decided that the interests of peace were better served by banning such demonstrations and restricting the group's rights of religious expression. And thus the group, called "The Temple Mount Faithful," was forbidden by the highest authority in the land to demonstrate at the Western Wall, which lies just beneath the site of the Temple Mount and the Dome of the Rock.

At that, the group opted to demonstrate anyway about half a mile away. They prepared a large block of stone and announced that it would be anointed as the cornerstone of the new Temple. Rumors began to fly in the Arab community that there would be a massive Jewish rally for the rebuilding of the Temple and that the Israelis were actually going to march onto the Temple Mount and threaten the Dome of the Rock and the Al Aqsa Mosque, which also graces the Mount today.

In reality, The Temple Mount Faithful carried their stone to the Pool of Siloam, well beyond sight and earshot of the Mount, but the Palestinians went into a frenzy and rushed onto the sacred hill, determined to stop any action by Jewish zealots. They began throwing rocks off the Mount upon the worshipers at the Western Wall below. Israeli police were called in to quell the riot. They quickly ran out of rubber bullets and finally fired live rounds at the mob before order was restored. Seventeen people were killed, and in its wake the new phase of the *intifada* left Israel in a general uproar and with the UN calling for an investigation into the matter. Retribution killings by the Palestinians, especially stabbings of civilians, continue to this day. Some hold that the Palestinians' cheering as the missiles fell on Tel Aviv during the war was also in retribution of the Temple Mount event.

Bible readers realize that this unique situation—a group of Israelites wanting to express a religious desire to see the Temple Mount under Jewish control—is an echo of the first century. Events occurring at the ancient Temple Mount at that time finally caused the Roman siege of Jerusalem and the destruction of the Temple in A.D. 70. We are now living in such a world as our Lord predicted, where Temple Mount events literally have global repercussions.

STRANGE BEDFELLOWS

The new realities brought about by the Gulf War have caused some strange relationships to form in the world. Many were utterly shocked to see the Secretary of State of the United States meeting respectfully with the arch-terrorist Hafiz al-Assad of Syria, who has apparently taken over the mantle of Arab terrorism from Qaddafi of Libya. It was evidently deemed necessary to shore up the northern boundary of Iraq and be sure that Syria would cooperate with the other powers in their efforts against Saddam Hussein. It would appear that the price of serious cooperation was to allow Syria to settle the disruptions in Lebanon with its own dominating presence. At this writing, the Syrian army utterly controls Lebanon and thus has clear access to Israel's northern border. And, most unpredictable of all, the Soviet Union and the United States appeared to work together against Iraq in intelligence matters and at the UN, certainly an unprecedented relationship in modern times.

In addition to the new alliances, the unpredictable breaking of some relationships also surprised many people. When Hussein unleashed Scud missiles against noncombatant Israel, as well as against Saudi Arabia and the Persian Gulf states, the act was repulsive to the world. Though Iraq's obvious strategy was to rally the Arabs against their common enemy, Israel, the Arab nations did not buy it. We were treated to the amazing spectacle of Arab nations urging Israel to restrain its natural impulses to retaliate against Iraq and stay out of the war. There actually were muted compliments to Israel when it exercised restraint. The unprecedented cooperation between Israel and its Arab enemies gave rise to hopes that some new era of conciliation and compromise would come about in the Middle East as a fallout of the Iraq war.

Only time will tell the true significance of the new alliances and the strange bedfellows. Our conviction is that all of these events move the world inexorably nearer to the fulfillment of biblical prophecy and, in particular, to that initial major event, the coming Russian invasion of Israel. Nations obviously have been reconfigured into positions more in keeping with the way Ezekiel styled the invasion. And it is also clear that due to other present biblical signs of the end—famine, pestilence, earthquakes, betrayal, false prophets, false Christs, and the like—prophesied by our Lord in His Olivet discourse (Matthew 24:4-14), related events are on schedule for the soon-coming of the seven-year Tribulation. Bible believers are anticipating the rapture of the church and the cataclysmic events to come preceding the second coming of Christ to the earth and the inheritance of our new Kingdom.

9

Satan on the Battlefield:
The Armageddon

The Russian invasion of Israel, in all its horror and devastation, will be only a curtain raiser.

Men will achieve much more in the Armageddon. In this chapter we're going to talk about *war!*

This global catastrophe will involve the entire race of man. No nation will escape. It is within reason to expect a billion casualties. Jesus said that if He were to delay His return, during this conflict "no life would have been saved" (Matthew 24:22).

Our two world wars, and all that went before and since among the races and nations of mankind, will be regarded as so much petty quibbling compared to this grand finale. All of man's most sophisticated science and technology will be placed in the service of his most primal lusts. Power-maddened armies numbering in the hundreds of millions will fall upon the Holy Land and upon each other, and only the patient God of our creation will be able to stem the tide.

The Armageddon conflict grows out of the Russian invasion of Israel. There is a great deal of uncertainty on this particular prophetic point. That the Russian invasion will happen is clear, but just when and how it is juxtaposed with the other issues of the end times has raised some controversy.

The problem is the placement of the invasion itself. It precedes Armageddon, but it is not completely clear how *far* before it. Some hold it to be a part of Armageddon, and some have it very much before the great war. The accompanying chart shows that scholars have attempted to place the grisly work of Gog and Magog at almost every point along the future prophetic timetable.

The problem of comparing different prophets and scheduling, as it were, their different foreseen events on a future timetable has its hazards. There are very good arguments for each of the positions shown on the chart.

It is our conviction that the Russian invasion of Israel will take place at a point very close to the beginning of the Tribulation period—Daniel's seventieth week. That is the moment when the Antichrist comes forward with his solution to the tensions in the Middle East and his infamous covenant with Israel (Daniel 9:27).

Daniel's seventieth week is calculated to last seven years, during which the great end-time prophecies will run their course until the second coming of Christ to the earth. The indication by Ezekiel (Daniel's contemporary) that Israel will spend seven years gathering up the debris from the Russian invasion to use for fuel is a tempting corollary to the seventieth week.

Could Daniel's seventieth week and Ezekiel's seven years refer to the same time period? We think that view is highly plausible, and that is one of the reasons we suggest that the Russian invasion of Israel will occur somewhere near the beginning point of the Tribulation period.[1]

Possibly the annihilation of Russia as a military force will set the stage for the Antichrist's rise to power.

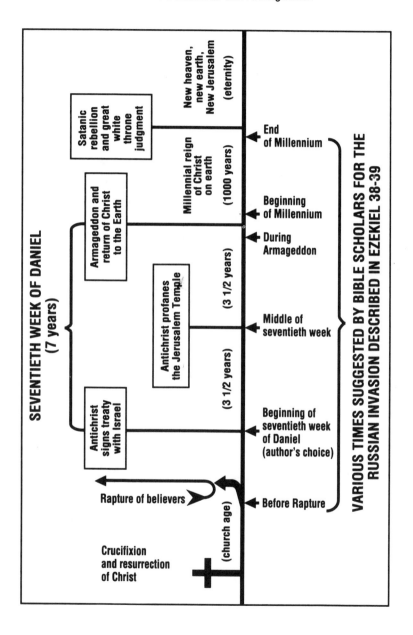

_.sents the revived Roman Empire, the ten-nation confederacy of Europe, and thus he would profit by the removal of that major rival for world domination. Israel would also be ripe for some peacemaker after the experience of the Russian invasion, even in victory.

Armageddon will come about through mismanagement by the Antichrist. He will first deliver on his promise to Israel; peace will prevail in the Holy Land for half of the Tribulation period—three and one-half years. During that period the Antichrist will set up an effective world domination, steadily gaining economic and political control over the nations. Everyone will buy and sell everything in accordance with the fiscal system of the Antichrist (Revelation 13:17), and even the very elect of God—the Jews—will be fooled by the calm before the storm.

Only in these days of computers and numerical designations, such as credit card and social security numbers, can we fully appreciate a world financial system. It used to take some imagination to see how the Antichrist could ever pull this off, but in these days of common currency and common markets it seems quite natural. In fact, it will seem like a great improvement over the past.

And perhaps it will be, in some ways, but the Antichrist will not be able to control his lust for power. When his total socio-politico-economic system is functioning on a worldwide scale, he will decide that he needs a title.

He will proclaim himself God!

It takes a special kind of egomaniac to choose that highest of titles. The Antichrist will not mean that he is like God, or has the virtual power of God over men; he will declare that he is God!

In 2 Thessalonians 2:4 the apostle Paul pictures that one-of-a kind blasphemy. "He takes his seat in the temple of God, displaying himself as being God."

The Antichrist will enter the Tribulation Temple, the third Jerusalem Temple, which will stand at this time, and plainly announce that he is God. Jesus specified that this "abomination of desolation," foreseen earlier by the prophet Daniel, would happen "in the holy place" of the Temple—the sacred sanctuary where God was said to dwell among His people (Matthew 24:15).

That incredible act will clearly identify the power behind the Antichrist. It is Satan's desire to replace God on earth; the Scriptures testify to that ongoing conflict since Satan's fall from heaven. The Antichrist will be Satan's most successful attempt to replace the Almighty. In the manner that God sent His Son to the earth, Satan will send the Antichrist, another resurrected "savior."

But the Jews have always regarded blasphemy as the highest of crimes, and they will recoil in horror from that action by their former mentor.

When Jesus identified Himself as the Son of God, there was much controversy among the Jews. The gospels tell of scenes of argument and whispered speculation about the remarkable Teacher of Galilee. The nation officially did not accept their Messiah, though enough Jews did that a church of Jerusalem was founded and the Word was promulgated to the world.

But this time—the Antichrist's time—there will be no such controversy. Israel will revolt.

From that moment on, the Antichrist's uneasy world peace will be shattered. The blasphemy occurs at the midpoint of the seven-year Tribulation period, so that three and one-half years are left to the mobilizations, invasions, and conflicts of the world armies leading up to the ultimate battle of Armageddon. The collision course is set when the Antichrist enters the Temple and proclaims himself God. He will become Satan on the battlefield.

Daniel chronicles an attack by kings of the north and south against the Antichrist in Israel. Apparently, once the fragile peace is ruined, men will at once resort to their former ways. Israel's revolt will show the Antichrist to be less than supernatural and may inspire widespread revolution against the dictator. Perhaps the attacking powers will consider the Antichrist's hold on things to be weakened by the Israeli revolt.

In any case, "the king of the South will collide with him, and the king of the North will storm against him with chariots, with horsemen, and with many ships," says Daniel (11:40). The Antichrist will have his hands full.

Many competent interpreters of prophecy have equated this king of the north with Ezekiel's Gog, who perpetrated the Russian invasion. That is one of the controversies existing about just when the Russian invasion occurs in the scheme of things. Naturally, if the king of the north is Gog, then the Russian invasion would occur after the Antichrist's blasphemy, or after the half way point of the Tribulation period. The king of the north reacts to Israel's revolt.

But we are disinclined to equate these two invaders. Ezekiel's Gog comes from the "uttermost north," and Daniel's king of the north is discussed in connection with his prophecies about the Greco-Syrian powers. We have already seen that Russia fits best the description of Gog's land for many reasons. In considering the king of the north, we must take into account Daniel's context. Daniel discusses, in chronological order, the four powers of Bible history, and his king of the north comes up in connection with the third such power—the Greco-Syrian power. Daniel 11:40-45 describes a purely Middle Eastern conflict, closer to home than the allied powers that descend in the invasion of Ezekiel 58 and 59.

Thus we are persuaded that the Russian invasion is separate from, and previous to, the invasion of the king of the north. As we understand the scenario, it will be Syria, united with Egyptian powers (the king of the south), who will attack the Antichrist and Israel.

Again, we do not sound very revolutionary to suggest that someday Egypt and Syria will mount a simultaneous attack against Israel.

But let us give credit where it is due. Daniel said it twenty-six centuries ago!

The present Middle Eastern conflicts are not to be confused with these future prophetic events, of course, but we can certainly see the stage being set. What an advantage we have over commentators of the past who could not even see an Israeli nation (before 1948), let alone these alliances and invasions. If we live long enough, we will see all prophecy fulfilled.

This invasion by the kings of the north and south ignites the whole of the world. The Antichrist will call upon his Western forces, the ten-nation confederacy of Europe, and the kings of the East (probably the massive hordes of China) will join in.

That will be a dramatic moment! From what we can gather, a 200-million-man army will march to the scene of the conflict in Israel from the east (Revelation 9:16).

The mighty Euphrates River, which would present an obstacle to a marching army from the east, will be dried up in the end times, according to prophecy. The Asian horde, nearly as large as the entire population of the United States, will wreak havoc on this terrible venture. They will account for the wiping out of a third of the earth's population (Revelation 9:18).

It all becomes very reasonable, if terrifying. Two hundred million soldiers was an unthinkable number at the time John wrote his astonishing book of Revelation, but China today would be able to field such an army. And uniquely, although China is the only power who could assemble such numbers, she is not equipped to transport them by mechanized means. If China seriously wanted to invade the Middle East, she would indeed be obliged to *walk* there. She does not have the ships and planes for transporting any sort of large army, let alone the behemoth foreseen by John.

So these are the combatants: the kings of the east, north, and south, and the European confederacy of the Antichrist. Israel will be stage-center as usual; she won't have to travel anywhere to participate in this war.

Russia will have already been neutralized by the stunning catastrophe of the earlier invasion of Israel. As for the other nations, the world is too small to escape the holocaust. The United States, not specifically mentioned in prophecy, will likely either be allied with the European confederacy (such as now in NATO) or be a helpless casualty of global thermonuclear effects. Those are suggested by repeated descriptions of raining fire, brimstone, smoke, and so on found in connection with these final conflicts.

THE BATTLE OF ARMAGEDDON

It's not quite clear who fights with whom about what. Getting there, as we have seen, is half the war.

Armageddon is different from what we have experienced in the history of our wars, not just in its scope but in its quality of supernatural events. Utilizing the same source—the Bible, which gives all the events leading up to this battle (and all of the' fulfilled prophecy of the past), we find a curious story replete with divine actions.

Zechariah covers the action of the war and gives in ominous tones the perennial hazards of making war on Jerusalem and Israel: "Behold, I am going to make Jerusalem a cup that causes reeling to all the people around; and when the siege is against Jerusalem, it will also be against Judah. And it will come about in that day that I will make Jerusalem a heavy stone for all the people; all who lift it will be severely injured. And all the nations of the earth will be gathered against it" (12:2-3).

All those who tangle with Jerusalem will be "cut in pieces" indeed. Despite the best efforts of the world's most capable and fanatic invaders through four thousand years of bloody conflict, Jerusalem has survived; and it will continue to survive.

The huge world forces come together where they have room to do their fearsome work—in the valley of Megiddo in quiet Galilee. In that valley, "called in the Hebrew tongue Har-Magedon" (Revelation 16:16), untold millions of soldiers armed with the ultimate weapons of war will stage mankind's most effective attempt at suicide. Blood will flow, according to Revelation, "up to the horses' bridles" (14:20).

Jerusalem, nearly one hundred miles away from the combat zone, will not be spared the effects of this horrifying conflict. Zechariah laments, "The city will be captured, the houses plundered, the women ravished, and half of the city exiled" (Zechariah 14:2). Considering the pure numbers of the invading forces, no portion of little Israel will be safe from actual combat. And Jerusalem, God's city, veteran of invasions, rapings, and lootings from time immemorial, will have to endure this one last catastrophe.

But in this final hour of terrible conflict, something miraculous will transpire among the people of Israel. Pressed to the wall, the Promised Land torn apart in vicious war, their historic fears of national annihilation coming to reality before their eyes, the Jews turn to God. They have always done this, but in this case they turn to their Messiah—at last! It seems that the testimony of the

144,000 Hebrew Christians, who minister on earth after the rapture and who share their faith in Christ, at last gets a hearing in Israel.

Jesus said clearly enough, "No one comes to the Father, but through Me" (John 14:6), and the Jews, in a time when their need to come to the Father is greater than ever before, will turn to their native Son, the carpenter of Nazareth. Jesus will be accepted as the true Messiah of Israel.

Isaiah 53, the conscience of the Jewish people, will be read with new understanding in Israel. "He was despised and forsaken . . . and like one from whom men hide their face, . . . and we did not esteem Him. . . . But He was pierced through for our transgressions, He was crushed for our iniquities" (vv. 3, 5). Whether out of the desperation of the tragic moment, or from the testimony of the Christian witnesses, or from a national realization that disaster has ever followed the Jews since the time of Christ, the Jewish nation will completely awake to Christ. They will finally say, "Blessed is the one who comes in the name of the Lord."

That is the password to salvation for the Jews. Jesus told them, while He was on the subject of the destruction of Jerusalem in His prophecy (Matthew 23:37-39), that He would not return until they welcomed Him in the words of Psalm 118:26: "Blessed is the one who comes in the name of the LORD."

It will be the greatest spiritual awakening in all of history, as the Jews come to Christ by the millions. It will be a true Day of Atonement in Israel: "In that day a fountain will be opened for the house of David and for the inhabitants of Jerusalem, for sin and for impurity (Zechariah 13:1). "And thus all Israel will be saved" (Romans 11:26).

God is practical. He promised deliverance to Israel when the nation was faithful. He demonstrated that in

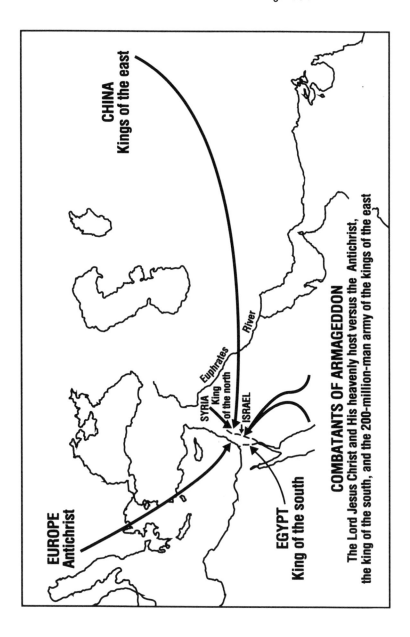

CHINA
Kings of the east

EUROPE
Antichrist

Euphrates
SYRIA
King
of the north
River

ISRAEL

EGYPT
King of the south

COMBATANTS OF ARMAGEDDON
The Lord Jesus Christ and His heavenly host versus the Antichrist,
the king of the south, and the 200-million-man army of the kings of the east

bringing His chosen out of Egypt in a miraculous deliverance in the time of Moses. He will do no less in the time of Armageddon.

The Jews receive Christ in a moment, as it were. There is no time to build a lot of churches or to ponder a lot of Scripture when Armageddon is going on in your land. The nation is saved as a nation, instantaneously, and on the battlefield. It is as if an electric current of truth is shot through everyone at once.

God's rewards are immediate.

The tide of Armageddon changes abruptly as the Lord imbues Israel with newfound military strength. The weakest buck private in the field will fight like King David, and the generals will be like God in battle: "In that day the LORD will defend the inhabitants of Jerusalem, and the one who is feeble among them in that day will be like David, and the house of David will be like God. . . . And it will come about in that day that I will set about to destroy all the nations that come against Jerusalem" (Zechariah 12:8-9).

The Israelis have been tough before, in the Six-Day War and the Yom Kippur War, but the world hasn't seen anything yet. The Lord Himself will come to lead His people in this final world war. "Then the LORD will go forth and fight against those nations, as when He fights on a day of battle. And in that day His feet will stand on the Mount of Olives" (Zechariah 14:3-4).

Jesus will return to His beloved Mount of Olives, adjacent to the Temple site, where He used to retire in the evenings for His own prayers. And cataclysmic things will happen. Militarily, those who attack Jerusalem are in for a bad time of it, to say the least. "The LORD will strike all the peoples who have gone to war against Jerusalem; their flesh will rot while they stand on their feet, and their eyes will rot in their sockets, and their tongue will rot in their mouth" (Zechariah 14:12).

John's Revelation sees a magnificent scene of Jesus arriving on a white horse at the head of a heavenly army: "And I saw heaven opened; and behold, a white horse, and He who sat upon it is called Faithful and True; and in righteousness He judges and wages war. . . . And the armies which are in heaven, clothed in fine linen, white and clean, were following Him on white horses" (19:11, 14).

Revelation 19 goes on to picture fowls eating the flesh of kings, captains, and mighty men. The Antichrist "and the kings of the earth and their armies" (v. 19) attempt war with Christ and His heavenly troops, with predictable outcome. John sees no scenes of lengthy battle, and Revelation goes immediately to the disposal of the Antichrist and his schemes for world domination in the "lake of fire" (v. 20).

The troops of the Antichrist, who represent, of course, the enormous armies of the Gentile nations of the world, are "killed with the sword which came from the mouth of Him who sat upon the horse, and all the birds were filled with their flesh" (v. 21).

This supernatural ending to the battle of Armageddon is not new in biblical accounts. We may say that there are natural wars and supernatural wars in connection with Jewish history, which is the story of a people whose destiny is controlled by God. (The deliverance of the Jews from Egypt showed the loss of the Egyptian forces when they tried to cross the Red Sea on the dry land used by the Jews.)

David experienced a supernatural victory over Goliath in response to his faithfulness. Joshua demolished the walls of Jericho with trumpets. The Maccabees experienced the miraculous touch of God when they defeated Antiochus and rededicated the second Temple.

Armageddon follows suit, demonstrating that God responds to true faith. When the Gentile nations first march against the Holy Land, they certainly have no fear of the little Israeli army. They plunder Jerusalem and set up their bloodletting in Galilee, indifferent to the great people whose land they desecrate.

But what a different story when the Jews turn to Christ! How shocking for the Gentiles to suddenly face an army of King David's with Jesus Christ at the head of it!

We have not experienced a supernatural war for some time. The Russian invasion of Israel, with its strange annihilation of the invading forces, is the first of this final period. On that occasion the issue is atheism versus faith in God, and as we have seen, God takes a hand in it. It is almost a smaller picture of the vicious Armageddon to follow.

Armageddon is the end of war. It marks the return of Jesus to the earth for an extended stay and a new kingdom. The great age of "peace on earth, good will toward men" is ushered in at the climax of Armageddon.

In a later chapter, we will take an encouraging look at the happier times provided by the return of Jesus Christ to the earth.

NOTE

1. For a complete analysis of the prophecy of the Tribulation period and the actions of the Antichrist in connection with it, see Thomas McCall and Zola Levitt, *Satan in the Santuary* (Chicago: Moody, 1973).

10

"The End Is Not Yet": Ezekiel's War and Armageddon

AN IMPORTANT DISTINCTION

In His prophetic discourse on the Mount of Olives, in answer to His disciples' question, "What shall be the sign of thy coming, and of the end of the world?" our Lord referred to a time of cataclysmic events. There would be unmistakably dramatic signs of impending disaster, He said, and He advised His disciples, "All these things must come to pass, but the end is not yet" (Matthew 24:3-6, KJV).

Our times are full of "signs of the end," according to many commentators, but the end itself is another matter. For biblical prophecies to be satisfied all elements must be completely in place and the ensuing actions exactly in accordance with those predicted by the prophets. The Lord's first coming, for example, satisfied some three hundred prophecies, many of them meticulously detailed, so Bible believers are perfectly certain of the identity of the Messiah. But historically, those who tended to read the Scriptures less precisely sometimes followed false messiahs; thus we must exercise care not to fall into such error.

In today's world, the term *Armageddon* is tossed around with abandon because of seemingly catastrophic situations far and wide. The idea of World War III's being just around the corner is a popular notion that has sold a great many newspapers. But students of prophecy understand the battle of Armageddon to be truly "the war to end all wars" (as World War I was erroneously called). Armageddon does not directly come out of any situation we see around us today and, most important, it is not to be confused with the coming Russian invasion of Israel, a completely different war.

Authors like to think that they are contributing to the overall body of information on their topic, but it is difficult and also hazardous to interpret Scripture in some new way in view of its very longevity. For two thousand to thirty-five hundred years theologians have commented on the Word of God, and it is consequently not a simple matter to contribute to that vast body of information. It would seem that everything that could be said has been said. On the other hand, as world events progress, those interpreters later in time can see more around them that may hint at a coming fulfillment or a more exact understanding of prophecy.

Also, scholarship in general, including that of Scripture, has improved in recent times. Probably in our own generation interpreters of prophecy have added a great deal that is of value to older interpretations of key prophecies. The original text of this book, *The Coming Russian Invasion of Israel*, offered the Christian reading public and all those who were interested in such matters a new slant on how the war described in Ezekiel's prophecy of the invasion of Gog and Magog could or should be understood. The interpretation was not entirely original with us, but we think we have brought the issue into the spotlight of public attention and have clarified a longtime controversy. The primary concept we have put forward is that the war in Ezekiel 38-39 is not Armageddon, but is different and distinct.

The Ezekiel war, which we call the coming Russian invasion of Israel (or the Russian invasion, for short), will occur, as we have said, either at the beginning of the Tribulation or just before it begins, whereas the war of Armageddon is at the very end of that period. Therefore, a considerable period of time is involved, since the Tribulation period is seven years long. Our reasons for making that distinction are given in earlier chapters of this book. We showed that there were several predominant views about the timing of the Ezekiel war, the most popular being that it was about the same as Armageddon. But we were convinced that the two wars must be considered separate events distinguished by time and character.

The importance of the timing of the Russian invasion has to do with whether or not we can connect the signs we are seeing today with the fulfillment of that prophecy. Put simply, if we believe the Russian invasion to be at the beginning of the Tribulation, then probably we can observe the stage being set for just such a conflict; if we believe it is a part of Armageddon, then before it happens a great amount of prophetic fulfillments would have to take place in addition to the signs we can now see. We would have to observe the meteoric ascendance to power of the Antichrist, his desecration of the Temple, and his subsequent persecution of Israel, for example, before we could reasonably expect to see Ezekiel's war.

But we firmly believe that the Russian invasion is something that comes out of the more immediate framework of the world we see before us. And since we believe that the rapture of the church must occur before the Tribulation, and that the Russian invasion must also occur just before or at the beginning of that seven-year period, then those two events appear to be connected in time. We are firmly committed to the pre-Tribulation rapture view, which teaches that the Lord will return for His own and take us back triumphantly to heaven before the dreaded Tribulation. We therefore hold that the return of the Lord is imminent and could occur at any moment.

The rapture is not dependent on some prophetic event that must occur before it; it is a free-floating surprise: "In the twinkling of an eye" (1 Corinthians 15:52), "as the lightning comes from the east" (Matthew 24:27). The Lord could literally come now—today—for His own; or, on the contrary, the Lord could wait until tomorrow, next year, or a century from now. One of the paradoxes of the Christian faith is that we must live as though He may come today, and we also have to plan and build with regard to the possibility that He may not come back for some time. We live with that contradiction by faith and not by sight (see Hebrews 11:1).

A SCENARIO OF LAST TIMES EVENTS

But in a scenario in which the rapture and the Russian invasion might take place in tandem, we can at least observe what we may interpret as preparations for the Russian invasion. We may thus be watchful for the rapture as we are commanded in Scripture: "But you, brethren, are not in darkness, that that day should overtake you like a thief; for you are all sons of light and sons of day. We are not of night nor of darkness; so then let us not sleep as others do, but let us be alert and sober" (1 Thessalonians 5:4-6).

Let us suppose, for instance, that the world once again finds itself embroiled in a Middle East crisis. This time the focus is not on the aggressive actions of Iraq but on the presumed aggressive action of Israel with reference to the West Bank, the Palestinians, or Israel's several surrounding enemies. And let us suppose that the Security Council of the United Nations decides to follow its precedent and invoke stern resolutions insisting that the Jewish nation withdraw from the occupied lands or face the severest consequences. Further, let us suppose that Israel stands firm, refusing to budge from what it considers to be both its biblically given land and its irreducible lines of defense. In that case, the Security Council would not countenance any disobedience to its dictates, and the United States, for various reasons, would be compromised to the extent that it could not or would not come to the aid of its client state. Europe and Japan would be paralyzed, as they were during the Yom Kippur War in 1973, and they would be terrified that their sources of oil might be totally disrupted if the Arab nations were not appeased in the matter.

In fact, the Western powers may well be advised to observe on the sidelines as Russia, Iran, Eastern Europe, and certain African powers attempt to resolve the intractable problem once and for all. Although those powers sat on the sidelines during the Persian Gulf War, they will be the true antagonists during this future war, and the former coalition may well be asked to sit it out.

And let us finally suppose also that the rapture of the church occurs at that very moment in our suggested scenario. The Lord returns for His own, the dead in Christ rise, and we who are then alive in Him are suddenly transformed and taken to be with Him forever (1 Thessalonians 4:16-18). What effect would the rapture have on the course of world events? In some countries there are not enough believers in Christ for it to make much difference at all. A relative handful of people disappearing would scarcely cause a blip on the local economy. In other countries it would cause quite a stir as thousands of people in responsible positions seemed to suddenly vanish into thin air. How would the rapture of the believers affect the United States if it occurred in the near future?

We have always supposed that in this Christian nation there are quite a number of believers in positions of leadership in economics, industry, government, and the military throughout the country. The nation might well be thrown into considerable confusion and temporary paralysis when the rapture occurs.

Moving along with our scenario, the Security Council would be on the verge of taking severe punitive action against Israel; the United States would be, at least temporarily, distracted and unable to come to Israel's aid; and Japan and Europe would be neutralized from taking any decisive action. In the midst of all that confusion Russia could easily rise to the occasion and, together with Eastern Europe, Persia, Ethiopia, and Libya, form a coalition force presumably capable of crushing the military power of Israel and removing it as an irritant on the world scene.

The invading forces come en masse against Israel, but to their horror they are met with a retaliation of such ferocity that they are decimated. The land of Israel is strewn with the decomposing bodies of its latter-day enemies, and Israel is miraculously delivered from the hands of its oppressors, just as the ancient prophet foretold some twenty-five centuries ago.

With the rapture of the church occurring at just that time, there would be no biblically educated spokesman to protest the Antichrist's claim that he has somehow protected Israel in that massive invasion. The Antichrist takes his cue and deals with a shaken and nervous Israeli government following the attempted invasion. He seems to claim credit for somehow protecting Israel from its enemies, and, as the prophet Daniel informs us, that evil "prince that shall come" (the Antichrist) will sign a treaty with Israel for seven years, during which he will presumably assure Israel of ongoing protection from its surviving enemies. The basis for that assurance may well be his claim that he caused the deliverance of Israel in the latest war. "I protected you this time, and I can protect you in the future with my powerful ten-nation confederacy in Europe," the Antichrist apparently promises.

But how could Israel suddenly shift from praising God for His power in overcoming the invading hordes of Magog and its allies (as Ezekiel prophesied) to recognizing the Antichrist as the protector of its destiny? That is truly a remarkable development from where we stand, but it is not unheard of in the long history of man in general and of Israel in particular. The apostle Paul, in his study of the Gentile world in Romans 1, indicates that man knew much of the glory of God but turned away from that awesome truth to worship mere animals and idols instead—praising creatures instead of the Creator. In a similar misjudgment, Israel, who had experienced the heady joy of the Exodus and the victorious crossing of the Red Sea, suddenly started worshiping a golden calf as the God that had brought them out of Egypt (see Exodus 32). Similarly, it seems that Israel in the last days, having escaped the horror of the invasion, puts itself under contract to the apparently beneficial domain of that "son of perdition." That misjudgment leads Israel and the rest of the world into the Tribulation and all of its disasters, culminating in Armageddon.

The scenario given above is merely a suggestion, of course. We are not prophets, nor the sons of prophets, but are simply endeavoring to interpret the revealed Word of God. Other scenarios are possible for the Russian invasion, and there are other reasons for Israel to sign up with the Antichrist. (Some have suggested that largely secular Israel, shocked by the attempted invasion, will simply be scared enough to "deal with the devil." Or perhaps Israel will have exhausted its weaponry in the invasion. Some suggest that Israel will use its nuclear arsenal in a last-ditch effort to defend itself, as we indicated in our original text. It would then be forced to turn to the Antichrist for military aid in the event of another invasion.)

However those things will happen, they will all happen. The rapture, the Russian invasion, the Tribulation, and Armageddon will all come to pass because they are all prophesied. But the order of events, the motivations of the nations for what they do, and the exact scenario by which all of it comes to pass is, of course, less certain and a matter of speculation by Bible analysts. And therein lies a certain amount of confusion and controversy, as will always be the case when mere men try to probe the mind of God.

A HISTORY OF CONFUSION

Sometimes unbelievers scoff at what they consider confusion among Bible students about what Scripture really says. And, in fact, readers of God's Word, even the most faithful of them, do come up with different conclusions about matters of doctrine and, particularly, prophecy. It is no secret that Judaism and Christianity, the biblical faiths, are fragmented and always have been to some degree. On the other hand, the biblical story is available to literally a whole world of people and has attracted many different kinds of adherents; some degree of disagreement is to be expected and is probably reasonable and healthy.)

Where prophecy is concerned, some Bible believers consider the placing of events in time to be hairsplitting. The issues of the relative timing of the rapture, the Tribulation, the Millennium, and such matters as the warfare described in the books of Ezekiel, Daniel, and the book of Revelation are considered arcane. "God will work it all out," they say, and it is not their concern. The theology becomes abstract and sometimes downright controversial. In the discussion about premillennialism and amillennialism, for example, some believers take a good-humored view they call "pan-millennialism" (it will all "pan out" in the end). But viewpoints like that one indicate almost an indifference to biblical truth, or a weariness on the part of those who should "not become weary" (Isaiah 40:31). The gospel story is clear enough, and they have adopted that, but the other thousand pages of truth in the Bible become opaque to those unwilling to probe for the treasures of the complete plan of God. The world of unbelievers may not be interested in what God has revealed about the human condition—history, prophecy, law, grace, and so forth—but it is essential that those of us who have staked our eternal destinies on the truthfulness of the Word of God endeavor to understand all of its disclosures.

The meticulous reasonings of the apostle Paul are a good example to those of us "upon whom the ends of the ages have come" (1 Corinthians 10:11). It seemed to be part of Paul's ministry virtually to dissect the known Word of God (the Old Testament) and to clarify it for the churches he established and served indefatigably. "Behold, I tell you a mystery" (1 Corinthians 15:51-57) he was given to saying in his zeal to increase the understanding of his followers in the early church.

We intend that kind of detailed presentation as we analyze the revelation of the Bible concerning future prophecy. Some 10 percent of Scripture deals specifically with predictions that have not yet been fulfilled, and that is a great deal of information. To put it in dimensional terms, unfulfilled prophecy would make about a 100-page book of very small type, in the particularly economical and efficient syntax of the inspired writers of Scripture. The Bible is a concise book, jam-packed with meticulous detail, and a goodly portion of its forecasts have not yet happened. Our task in updating Ezekiel's prophecy is to correlate all of the details given—every word of every verse—in a way that is accurate and understandable to our readers. If we have more finely split hairs than those hairsplitters who have preceded us, then perhaps we have accomplished our purpose.

On the general subject of warfare in the end times, Scripture is replete. Daniel, Zechariah, Ezekiel, and the book of Revelation are full of that information. It must be recognized that the second coming of Christ to this earth is not preceded by tranquillity but by an all-consuming orgy of international conflict. The purpose of *The Coming Russian Invasion of Israel* was to analyze the many descriptions of warfare, to identify as best we could the combatants, and to establish a reasonable chronology of those events. Our thesis in the end was that the war described in Ezekiel was quite similar to, but distinctly different from (and much prior to), the warfare revealed in the other end-times war prophecies, those concerning Armageddon.

DIFFERENCES BETWEEN EZEKIEL'S WAR AND THE WAR OF ARMAGEDDON

Choosing the nation of Russia as Magog was not original with us, but the identity of Magog has been confused by analyses that combine Ezekiel's invasion and the war of Armageddon. As we have said elsewhere in this book, those who believe that Ezekiel's war is identical to that described in Daniel, Zechariah, and Revelation tend to make Gog of Magog the same as the king of the North in Daniel. Russia's distinctive role given in Ezekiel becomes confused with the general invasion of Israel perpetrated by virtually all the armies of the earth as part of Armageddon. All end-times warfare, they say, occurs at the end of the Tribulation period as part of the vast final battle.

Many a theological writer before us had some difficulty correlating the events described in Ezekiel's war with the prophecies concerning Armageddon. It just seemed that so many of the details of Ezekiel would not fit with what the other prophecies revealed. Expositors tended to gloss over details, experiencing discomfort even as they taught.

A point of difficulty was Israel's activities in the aftermath of Ezekiel's war. The Jewish nation will undertake seven months of burial of the dead and seven years of frugal burning of debris from the war (saving precious trees and fossil fuels of which Israel has so little). The problem is, if Ezekiel's war were the same as Armageddon and thus occurred at the return of Christ to the earth to establish His Kingdom, those activities on Israel's part do not seem consistent with the glory, joy, and bounty associated with the return of the Messiah.

The cast of characters is similar but crucially different in the two wars, as well. Ezekiel's concise list of Magog and its allies—Persia, Ethiopia, Libya, Gomer, and Beth-togarmah—constitute the whole of the invasion, but Zechariah 12-14 describes Armageddon as a war in which "all the nations of the earth" will come against Jerusalem (12:3). That distinction is critical. One should not gloss over the difference between being attacked by a half-dozen nations and being invaded by the "whole world" (more than 150 nations). The two wars actually are more like two similar dramas with different actors. They are also plays of wholly different magnitude, as well. Compared to the grand opera of Armageddon, the coming Russian invasion of Israel is merely a play of one act.

The ways in which the Lord chooses to intervene in the two wars are quite different also. In the Russian invasion, the Almighty disrupts the battle by means of an earthquake and fire raining down from heaven (see Ezekiel 38:19-23). Those verses have inspired many to consider that small but devastating conflict to be a nuclear exchange. In any case, it seems to be God in heaven, and not Israel, who repulses the enemy. Armageddon, however, is fought by Christ personally, returning with His saints and bringing about the national conversion of Israel, who will "look upon [Him] whom they have pierced" (Zechariah 12:10). The instantly converted Israeli believers will be able to fight the enemy with supernatural power. Ordinary soldiers will fight like King David, and the officers will fight like angels. In addition, the invading enemy will be visited by a terrible plague that will, in the scriptural description, cause the flesh to fall off their bones.

And finally, the outcome of the two wars will be different. The hills of Israel will be covered with the dead bodies of the invading armies, and the land will be literally poisoned. Burial crews will evidently work around the clock for seven months to bury the dead. The ordinary citizens and even the tourists will be asked to mark the spots where they see bodies that must be dealt with by the buriers. And, of course, the use of enemy weaponry as fuel, sparing the trees that have been so painstakingly planted in the revived homeland, will be part of the outcome as well. Ezekiel supplies that that fuel will last the Israelis exactly seven years, precisely the length of the Tribulation period. Our conviction is that that period of time is no coincidence, but a clear indication that the Russian invasion will have taken place by the beginning of the Tribulation.

The aftermath of Armageddon is a different matter altogether. When Christ returns to terminate that final war, He will take charge not only concerning the disposition of His enemies but also in the matter of establishing His Kingdom on the earth. He will judge the nations, as He indicates in Matthew 25:31-46, and then permit saved

Israel and the Gentiles who are "sheep" (those who demonstrated their faith in Christ during the seven years) to enter into His Kingdom, joining the resurrected saints of both the church age and the Old Testament era. That triumphant, joyful establishing of a new government and building of a new house of the Lord in Jerusalem is extremely different from the difficult times following the Ezekiel war.

SIMILAR BUT DIFFERENT

To briefly restate the theological dilemma with which our book deals primarily, we should emphasize the similarities and differences of the two prophetic wars of the Tribulation era. They are similar in that both Armageddon and the Russian invasion are wars specifically against Israel. The nations that come against Israel in both cases are determined to annihilate the revived chosen nation of the Lord in the end times. In both cases the enemies of the Lord appear overwhelming in their combined strength, much as Goliath appeared in his confrontation with the teenage David. And finally, the results of both wars are similar. The aggressive invaders are destroyed supernaturally by divine intervention, and Israel is seen to be the victor over its massed attackers. God is perceived as having provided miraculous victories in both wars.

But in numerous ways the two wars are crucially different. The protagonists are different, the manner of the Lord's intervention is critically different, and the outcomes of the two wars are wholly different.

It is notable that no theological scholarship or worldly event has come along in the nearly twenty years since the publication of *The Coming Russian Invasion of Israel* to suggest any difference in those distinctions. The principle of two different wars as widely separated in time as is possible in the Tribulation period (seven years) seems intact and, of course, it makes a difference. As we alluded earlier, if one believes that Ezekiel's war is part of Armageddon, then developments on the world scene today are only vaguely connected to that great war since it is more than seven years away and demands a reconfiguring of nations of some magnitude before it comes about. But if one thinks of the Russian invasion as virtually the next prophetic event (after or simultaneous with the rapture of the church), then current events have an entirely new urgency and the alliances we are seeing today represent the required reconfiguration of nations for Ezekiel's war.

And if Ezekiel's war is coming right up, then the rapture is that much sooner. Nothing makes more of a difference to believers than that.

11

"Babylon the Great Is Fallen!"
Revelation 18:2

Revival of Interest in Babylon

We might say that Babylon, an ancient empire centered in what is roughly the territory of modern Iraq, had disappeared from world attention for some 2,200 years before Saddam Hussein. In ancient times, mighty Babylon competed with the enlightened and advanced empire of Egypt for a thousand years, vying for world dominance. Renowned sovereigns and occupiers alike administrated fearsome Babylon; names such as Nimrod, Hammurabi, Nebuchadnezzar, Cyrus, and Alexander the Great graced the lengthy annals of that singular power. For many, Babylon dictated life and death to the known world.

But in the past two millennia, when so many of the mighty fell, Babylon has been quiescent and until recently virtually forgotten as the emphasis of civilization shifted to Europe, Asia, and the Western Hemisphere. But the revival of world interest in the area can be credited to probably the least likely public relations man of the latter half of the twentieth century, the "Butcher of Baghdad."

Saddam Hussein would like to think that he is profoundly influencing the course of world events, but he probably got more attention than he really wanted during the Persian Gulf War. And although he supposed himself a great religious, political, and military leader, it is likely he did not count on sending millions of Christians back to their Bibles to verify what the Scriptures really say about Babylon.

"MYSTERY BABYLON": THE SYMBOLIC VIEW OF REVELATION 17-18

The predominant view of Babylon among Christians for centuries was that it had been utterly destroyed by divine decree, never to rise again out of its ashes. Isaiah, in particular, was the prophet who enunciated the downfall of the great citadel: "And Babylon, the beauty of kingdoms, the glory of the Chaldeans' pride, will be as when God overthrew Sodom and Gomorrah. [Babylon] will never be inhabited or lived in from generation to generation; nor will the Arab pitch his tent there, nor will shepherds make their flocks lie down there" (Isaiah 13:19-20).

As we know from Daniel, the Persians swiftly conquered Babylon about 539 B.C. on the night Belshazzar held his great idolatrous feast and literally "saw the handwriting on the wall" (see Daniel 5:5, 13-28). Cyrus then ruled, at least for a time, from Babylon. But the last major world ruler to occupy Babylon was, strangely enough, the Greek conqueror Alexander the Great. Alexander came from Athens and Macedonia and took over practically the entire civilized world, from India to Egypt. When he returned to Babylon from his conquests, one would have thought that he would have been flushed with joy and exhilarated with power. Instead, he wept because there were no more worlds for him to conquer.

He died in Babylon in 333 B.C. in a spirit of deep depression.

We do not hear much about Babylon from then on. The apostle Peter wrote, "She who is in Babylon, chosen together with you, sends you greetings" (1 Peter 5:13), thus indicating that he was writing from the city of Babylon. Roman Catholic interpreters, as well as many others, have thought that Peter was writing cryptically and really meant, in a kind of Christian code, that he was writing from the city of Rome but did not want the Romans to know that he was there. That theory seems dubious in that the apostle Paul certainly did not hide the fact that he was in Rome when he wrote his letters from there. In view of there being no historical evidence that Peter visited Rome, we prefer to take the Scriptures literally.

Why would the "chief apostle" be in Babylon? Although Peter began his ministry in Jerusalem and ministered there in the mother church for a long time, he was certainly persecuted in Jerusalem and was imprisoned at least once. It is not surprising that Peter should have left Jerusalem to minister elsewhere. But where would he go? Paul says in Galatians 2 that he, Peter, and the church at Jerusalem reached an agreement about their respective ministries. Peter was the apostle to "the circumcision," the Jews, whereas Paul was to be the apostle to "the uncircumcision," the Gentiles. Thus, wherever Peter went outside of Jerusalem, it would certainly be for the purpose of concentrating on his specialty, Jewish evangelism.

Babylon was a good choice for Peter. During the first century there was a large Jewish population in that great Mesopotamian city. Jews had been there since the Babylonian captivity by Nebuchadnezzar. That ferocious conqueror had deported the two tribes of Judah, acquiring the prophets Daniel and Ezekiel in the bargain. Although many thousands of Jews wanted to return to Israel after the seventy years of forced exile, far more decided they would rather stay in the environs of Babylon than face the pioneer hardships of reestablishing Jerusalem. It is somewhat analogous to the situation of the Jews today in the twentieth century when, for a second time, Israel is returning to the land (the third time, if one counts the Exodus from Egypt following the 400-year sojourn in slavery). Only about 4 million Jews reside in Israel now, whereas the rest of the some 15 million Jews are in many countries throughout the world.

Therefore, it is altogether consistent with Peter's calling that when he had to leave Jerusalem he would have settled in Babylon, where such an important Jewish community resided. There he could minister for Christ among the Jewish people and encourage the church that had been established. Thus, the last we hear of this beloved Galilean fisherman is that he is serving his Lord in the ancient and renowned city of Babylon.

After the first century, Babylon continued to be a strong force for religion, though not Christianity. Rather, it was a focal point for the development of Judaism after the destruction of Jerusalem. When the Temple was destroyed by the Romans in A.D. 70, as Jesus had predicted, the Jews were scattered from Jerusalem. Many rabbis settled in Tiberias, on the western shore of the Sea of Galilee, and there, by the lake that was the center of the Messiah's marvelous ministry of teaching and miracles, the leaders of Judaism established a center of learning. In effect, they had to create a new Judaism based on the reality that there was no Temple, no priesthood, no sacrifice, and no shrine of Jerusalem. Here they codified the "Oral Law," which has come to be known as the Talmud. That 2,600-year-old written version of the oral tradition of scriptural commentaries and laws was completed around A.D. 600.

But there were really two Talmuds. The rival center of Jewish learning to Tiberias was none other than Babylon. Jewish scholars there enjoyed a long tradition of studious disputation, which had not been interrupted by revolt and devastating war against Rome, as had been the case in Jerusalem and throughout Israel. The Jewish sages in Babylon also set about to write down the "Oral Law," which had been passed down from generation to generation. Thus, there came to be the Jerusalem Talmud (compiled in Tiberias) and the Babylonian Talmud. It is almost universally agreed that the Babylonian Talmud is superior in authenticity and scholarship.

But in the Gentile world, Babylon faded from the world scene around the seventh century A.D., no longer a dominating world power but, rather, just a sort of regional "county seat," as it were, and a site of scholarly pursuits by its minority of Jews who still lived and worked there. Later the city fell into ruins and scarcely has been heard of since.

The situation of a completely extinct city mentioned in future prophecy has led many interpreters of the Scriptures to interpret Revelation 17-18 in a purely symbolic sense. Those two chapters speak of "Babylon" in the end times as a center of false religion and economic power that will be destroyed in apocalyptic fury. Not many scholars understood the reference to mean that the old city of Babylon would actually be rebuilt and thrive again in a Tribulation period setting. Instead, they have thought that those prophecies referred to the religious and economic character of the Tribulation era, which was symbolically referred to as Babylon. Thus, they have maintained a symbolic, and not a literal, interpretation of the Babylon of Revelation 17-18, and the true ancient city of Babylon was almost utterly forgotten, irrelevant under the sands of the Iraqi desert.

MODERN IRAQ AND THE NEW BABYLON

But in our time, thirteen centuries later, Babylon is found once again at the center of international attention. A strange and ruthless Arab despot has arisen in Iraq, which is roughly the geographical equivalent of ancient Babylonia, and he claims to be the new Nebuchadnezzar who will rebuild Babylon and conquer Israel. How truly amazing are such aspirations, especially to those of us who believe the Bible and look forward with anticipation to the return of Christ to the earth after just such preliminary events.

Before August 1990, most of us had scarcely given any thought to Iraq, much less to its neighbor Kuwait. Perhaps we had heard that it was one of those numerous Arab countries in the Middle East that had a lot of oil. Maybe we even knew that it had been gripped in an eight-year-long war with Iran, whom we considered the archenemy of the West in general and America in particular. Khomeini was the villain, as far as most of us were concerned, and the Iraqi strongman Saddam Hussein seemed to be the ideal force to keep in check Iran's expansionist ambitions throughout the Muslim world. That is apparently the way the Western governments saw things.

Then suddenly Iraq amassed its forces against Kuwait, invaded the little country, and forced the entire world into an exercise of international economic and military discipline the likes of which we have rarely seen. In addition, the nations of the earth were compelled to virtually psychoanalyze the peculiar personality of this modern day presumer to the throne and power of Nebuchadnezzar.

In 1987, when Iraq was still deeply entrenched in its debilitating war with Iran, Saddam Hussein held a gala tourist festival celebrating the first stages of his reconstruction of Babylon. He invited journalists, political leaders, and scholars from around the world to commemorate his considerable accomplishment of restoring from its ruins some of the most spectacular elements of the old city, including part of the wall, the famous Gate of Ishtar, and one of Nebuchadnezzar's palaces. Iraq even struck a coin featuring on one side the likeness of Nebuchadnezzar in the background and Saddam Hussein in the foreground, with cuneiform and English script commemorating the Babylon International Festival. There is no question that Hussein was not just creating a Middle Eastern Disneyland but was endeavoring to assert his authority as a new Nebuchadnezzar who would dominate that entire region, with all of its wealth and influence.

The restoration work on the city of Babylon and the power play by Iraq has forced many believers in the Bible to rethink their interpretation of the prophecies about Babylon in the Scriptures. Is Babylon indeed destroyed according to Bible prophecy, never again to be revived, or is there a future for the ancient city that has been ignored by Christian scholars for centuries?

RELIGIOUS AND COMMERCIAL BABYLON: THE LITERAL VIEW

Just as the Persian Gulf War was getting into full gear, a most provocative book appeared, *The Rise of Babylon*. The author, Charles H. Dyer, certainly struck a strong chord among those who were watching the nightly bombing raids on television. Modern Baghdad stands less than fifty miles from the revived artifacts and buildings of ancient Babylon.

Dyer's thesis was that the Babylon of Revelation 17-18 is not just symbolic of the religious and commercial apostasy of the Tribulation era, but that the old city of Babylon itself is destined to rise again and will be the religious and economic center of the Tribulation. We tend to concur with that view.

Just as Jerusalem, the city of the great King, must be revived in the end times, so its rival city, Babylon, must come to the fore in the last days. The point is that the prophecies of Isaiah and other prophets who predicted the utter demise of Babylon have not yet been fulfilled. Babylon was indeed captured by the Persians and continued steadily downhill as a great power, but it was never completely uninhabited. There were always people who lived there throughout all those centuries, and it could scarcely be said that the ancient city of Babylon had suffered a fate similar to Sodom and Gomorrah, as Isaiah predicted would ultimately happen to Babylon.

Thus we believe that Babylon has survived the ravages of time to fight another day, and it appears that it will again become a center of world attention with regard to religious worship and economic prowess.

REVELATION 17:
BABYLON THE HARLOT RELIGION

In chapter 17 of the book of Revelation, John is shown a spectacular vision of an alluring but drunk and decadent harlot. She is seen riding upon the Beast, who has elsewhere been identified as the Antichrist. Her name is "BABYLON THE GREAT, THE MOTHER OF HARLOTS" (v. 5). In fact, our first ancestor, Adam, used the phrase in regard to Eve, "the mother of all living" (Genesis 3:20). And here again, we find the phrase in Revelation, describing the infamous Mystery Babylon as the Mother of Harlots. She is described as intoxicated, but not with liquor; instead, she is drunk with "the blood of the saints, and with the blood of the witnesses of Jesus" (Revelation 17:6). Her intoxication comes from her wanton slaughter of believers in Christ.

Who is that monstrous woman, also described as "the great city, which reigns over the kings of the earth" (Revelation 17:18)? Who is the Mystery Babylon that consorts with the Antichrist and "rides him" into power in the last days and conspires to make war against the Lamb of God? We believe she is none other than the idolatrous religion of the new and revived Babylon of the days of the Tribulation.

False religion began in Babylon in the days of Nimrod and the Tower of Babel, and false religion will end there in the days of the Antichrist. Religion will certainly not cease to exist when the church is raptured to be with Christ. Instead, it will flourish and abound. It is probably accurate to say that the most devastating enemies of the gospel have not been the out-and-out atheists and criminals of the world but, rather, the apparently mild and respectable leaders of the religions of the world, whether they have a Christian or a purely pagan background. It is those upright citizens and dignified clerics and priests who have undermined the faith and endeavored to crush the message of God's redeeming grace and those who bear the message of that grace. From man's point of view they are fine, upstanding, moral people, but from God's point of view they are seen collectively as a drunken, unfaithful, filthy, murderous, and idolatrous harlot.

It appears that the predominance of the harlot over the Beast is short-lived, however. She rides on the Beast for a period of time, but ultimately the Beast turns on her, kicks her off, and actually devours her. The implications of that curious event are that when the Tribulation begins, the Antichrist and the Babylonian-centered false religion of the world cooperate in coming to international power. But eventually the Antichrist tires of the dominance of Babylon's religion. He casts it aside and declares his own religion, with himself as God. Such arcane activity is undoubtedly tied in with the Antichrist's takeover and desecration of the rebuilt Temple in Jerusalem: "[He] takes his seat in the temple of God, displaying himself as being God" (2 Thessalonians 2:4).

At any rate, Babylon appears to be in the forefront of formal religious activity at the early stages of the Tribulation. And we believe that the literal city of Babylon is meant, rather than a "Babylon" symbolic of idolatrous religion in general. Our view is that Scripture is to be understood literally, unless there is overwhelming evidence that it cannot be understood literally. After all, with the resurgence of the ancient city of Babylon on the Euphrates River, what is to prevent it from resuming its former dominance of world religion in the last days? Certainly the worldwide true Christian church will be long gone in the rapture and could not object.

Those who believe in the inerrant truthfulness of the Word of God must reckon on a real and literal rise of Babylon promoting formal religious activity in the latter days.

REVELATION 18:
BABYLON, THE CENTER OF INTERNATIONAL COMMERCE

The scene shifts in chapter 18 of Revelation. John is still presented with information about the future Babylon, but the focus is now on its sudden demise as an international commercial center:

> And the kings of the earth . . . will weep and lament over her, . . . saying, "Woe, woe, the great city, Babylon, the strong city! For in one hour your judgment has come." And the merchants of the earth weep and mourn over her, because no one buys their cargoes any more. (Revelation 18:9-11)

The rulers and the captains of industry of the Tribulation era become distraught because Babylon is instantly destroyed as a center of commerce. One is reminded of the economic boycott of Iraq during the Persian Gulf conflict. Such a fate for the city seems to justify the prophecy of Isaiah that Babylon would be destroyed like Sodom and Gomorrah. In all the long history of Babylon, a city as old as civilization itself, there has never been such a cataclysmic destruction of the city. For most of the past two millennia it was simply allowed to fade away into obscurity.

Most interpreters, again, have believed that that description of Babylon is symbolic of the world economic power in the end times, but could it not be understood literally as well? Is it unthinkable that the ancient city of Babylon could once again be rebuilt and become an economic power to be reckoned with during the Tribulation?

Our conviction is that just such an event was revealed to John. In light of the devastation Iraq endured during the Persian Gulf War, we may not fully understand how Saddam Hussein's aspirations for Babylon can be realized, but perhaps the enormous oil wealth of the Middle East could ultimately finance the reconstruction of Babylon and make it an economic miracle of the modern world. After all, who would have thought that Japan could emerge from the nuclear ashes of World War II and make Tokyo the economic center of the Far East? Such a restoration from the ruins of ancient Babylon seems possible to us, especially considering the great resources lying beneath the Arabian desert.

Thus, we anticipate the literal fulfillment of this prophecy, along with the other end times fulfillments.

12

"Thy Kingdom Come"

Jesus will not return strictly for His military mission. We can be thankful enough that the battle at Armageddon is stopped short of annihilating all mankind, but the Lord will return for a greater purpose. He will establish the first successful, peaceful, equitable world government. His will shall be "done in earth, as it is in heaven."

The inexorable series of cataclysmic events proceeding from the Russian invasion of Israel goes on, as Jesus occupies His throne of glory and confronts what is left of man's broken-down world.

HOW DID YOU TREAT MY BROTHERS?

First Jesus will judge the nations of the world—the Gentiles.

This will be quite a different Jesus from the sacrificial lamb of the gospels. The Savior, who endured humiliation, torture, and physical death at the hands of the unbelieving, will return as a Lion.

He had taught His followers to pray, "Thy kingdom come, Thy will be done, on earth as it is in heaven" (Matthew 6:10), and He will see to it that that prayer is answered at once.

Here is how things will stand as the Lord operates His office of immigration into the new kingdom: the Gentiles of the world, the survivors of Armageddon, will be judged; for two other groups the judgment process will be waived. One of those will be the unique group of past believers—those of Old Testament times and of the church age, along with those believers who died as martyrs in the Tribulation. They will be resplendent in their resurrection bodies. The remaining group will be the Christian nation of Israel.

As we have seen, all Israel will be redeemed at what looks to be its final hour. They will have carte blanche into the millennial kingdom, as will all other believers. As Paul exulted, "All Israel will be saved" (Romans 11:26).

And that takes care of everybody. The dividing line is Christ, who says, "If you are not for Me, you are against Me."

Israel will take its guaranteed place as "the head [of the nations] and not the tail" (see Deuteronomy 28:13). Jesus will judge and govern in Jerusalem, the new world capital in the Millennium. All the law of the world will emanate from Jerusalem as, in a way, it always did.

Now back to the Gentiles who will stand trial before Jesus. They will at least have a fair judge, but the issue of whether they have believed or not will have really caught up with them this time.

Jesus will ask, "How did you treat My brothers?" The beautiful chapter Matthew 25 gives a transcript of that future courtroom scene:

> But when the Son of Man comes in His glory, and all the angels with Him, then He will sit on His glorious throne. And all the nations will be gathered before Him; and He

will separate them from one another, as the shepherd separates the sheep from the goats; and He will put the sheep
on His right, and the goats on the left. (vv. 31-33)

Nobody gets to testify because, by the Lord's criteria,
all already have. After He separates the defendants into
the two groups,

> the King will say to those on His right, "Come, you who
> are blessed of My Father, inherit the kingdom prepared
> for you from the foundation of the world. For I was hun-
> gry, and you gave Me something to eat; I was thirsty, and
> you gave Me drink; I was a stranger, and you invited Me
> in; naked, and you clothed Me; I was sick, and you visited
> Me; I was in prison, and you came to Me." (vv. 34-36)

These defendants, the sheep, are incredulous. They
have never seen Jesus. They are honest enough to say so:

> Lord, when did we see You hungry, and feed You, or
> thirsty, and give You drink? (v. 37)

And they cover all the categories given above by the
Lord. They are not aware that they have greatly honored
the Lord by their right doings in the Tribulation period.
Jesus explains to them:

> Truly I say to you, to the extent that you did it to one of
> these brothers of Mine, even the least of them, you did it
> to Me. (v. 40)

The sheep receive full credit for their faith and acts
of love during the difficult time of the Antichrist.
Jesus' brethren are the Jews, particularly the 144,000
Jews who suffered the Tribulation period in unflinching
faith in the Lord and stalwart witnessing to the lost. In a
larger sense, all mankind are Jesus' brethren since He be-

came a man on our behalf. But the context here dictates the "brethren" in question as the Lord's fellow Jews.

Had the sheep been Bible students, they would not have been at all surprised at their acquittal in Jesus' courtroom. God says plainly in Genesis 12:3, at the stirring moment of the Abrahamic covenant, "I will bless those who bless you" (the Jewish nation). As we have seen, God's covenant with His chosen people is to endure to eternity. Jesus would not be expected to condemn those who blessed the Jews.

But God goes on to tell Abraham in that same Scripture, "And the one who curses you I will curse," and we now come to the goats, the defendants on Jesus' left.

They failed to exercise benevolence to those in need in the hard times. "For I was hungry, and you gave Me nothing to eat; I was thirsty, and you gave Me nothing to drink" (Matthew 25:42). They, too, question their judge: "When did we fail? When did we even *see* You?"

The Lord applies the same precedent:

> Truly I say to you, to the extent that you did not do it to one of the least of these, you did not do it to Me. (v. 45)

They couldn't ask for a fairer trial.

Their sentence is a hard one. They fare no better than the devil and his henchmen. "Depart from Me, accursed ones," pronounces the Lord, "into the eternal fire which has been prepared for the devil and his angels" (v. 41).

Admission to the millennial kingdom for Gentiles, then, rests on whether they demonstrated faith in Christ by showing kindness to the suffering chosen people in their final hour. There will be some Gentiles, then, who will go through the Tribulation, believe in Christ, and have their hearts in the right place toward the suffering; and so they will obtain a place in the kingdom. They will not become rulers, as age-of-grace Christians will, but they will become subjects in that glorious and peaceful world.

Is there really a person alive who cannot see the good of feeding the hungry, comforting the sick, and clothing the naked? Can Jesus' principles have been so covered over by a relentlessly wicked world that no one will respond in sympathy?

Hardly! The principle of salvation by faith is not relaxed at this remarkable litigation, but an individual might be spared for the smallest show of human mercy. And we all have the potential for mercy. We still are, after all, created in the image of God.

It won't be easy to assist the enemies of the Antichrist in such times. Obviously the punishment on earth will be severe for those who have anything to do with God or His chosen people. The Antichrist is "god" during the Tribulation, as he duly proclaims, and any valid worship of the true God would be a kind of inverse blasphemy.

On the other hand, opportunities to do the right thing will abound. The vocal 144,000 Hebrew Christian preachers will be a helpless target of the atheistic forces at large in the world. They will likely be jailed, left to go hungry, and otherwise abused. They will certainly need the kind of help the Lord specified for His brethren. At risk of death, courageous believers will still qualify, according to the Scriptures.

And that is how this first judgment day will proceed. Basically we have just two groups—believers, with a free pass into the kingdom, and unbelievers, who will flunk the entrance exam.

Where do you stand?

KING OF KINGS

Once the membership of the new kingdom is settled, it gets immediately underway.

Kingdoms on earth never really have worked out very well. Typically, the monarch connived and cheated behind the scenes while the people sang, "God save the king." But it's a completely different story when God is the King!

The sinless, compassionate, incorruptible King will make all the difference in the Millennium, despite the fact that, to some degree, men will still be up to their old tricks.

Isaiah gives us an unforgettable picture of the power and abilities of Jesus as King:

> For a child will be born to us, a son will be given to us; and the government will rest on His shoulders; and His name will be called Wonderful Counselor, Mighty God, Eternal Father, Prince of Peace. There will be no end to the increase of His government or of peace, on the throne of David and over His kingdom, to establish it and to uphold it with justice and righteousness from then on and forevermore. The zeal of the LORD of hosts will accomplish this. (9:6-7)

What was not entirely clear to the Jews who read their Scriptures was the two-phase appearance of Jesus on earth. The essence of Christianity—that there was to be first an appearance characterized by the Messiah's rejection and suffering—was overlooked, although it is prophesied clearly (and by the same prophet Isaiah):

> He was despised and forsaken of men, a man of sorrows, and acquainted with grief. . . . Surely our griefs He Himself bore, and our sorrows He carried. . . . But He was pierced through for our transgressions, He was crushed for our iniquities; the chastening of our well-being fell upon Him, and by His scourging we are healed. All of us like sheep have gone astray, each of us has turned to his

own way; but the LORD has caused the iniquity of us all to
fall on Him.) (53:3-6)

Somehow, though the kingship of the Messiah was
certainly realized by the Jews—they still expect their
kingly Messiah—His sacrifice aspect was missed, despite
this passage and many like it in the Old Testament. Alter-
nate interpretations for these revelations are given by
Jewish scholars. But as we have seen, the chosen people
are to come to the full realization of their Messiah's mission and will welcome Him as King. Their Promised
Land is to become truly the center of the earth.

The necessity of the delay between the Lord's two
comings was lost on the Jews, since their Old Testament
theology did not reveal a period like the church age. During that period, Christ reaches the world with His gospel.
The Jews, already the chosen people, have never felt that
they needed that special provision.

The church, as the body of believers reached during
the interim period is called, is to marry Jesus before He
assumes His earthly throne. John pictures that great wedding in heaven and refers to the church as the bride of
Christ (Revelation 19:7)

Following that, Jesus returns with His bride to the
earth and occupies His throne of David.

The Christians, then, are originally raptured, or
"caught up," to heaven to be with Jesus from the hard
times of the Tribulation period on earth, and then they
are wed to the Lord. Finally, they return with Him and
enjoy their promised privileges of ruling in the millennial kingdom. The population of the kingdom is completed when the Christians return with the Lord to join those
on the earth who have qualified for the kingdom by their
faith in Christ shown by their good works toward the
Lord's brethren in the Tribulation. The latter completely
qualify as true believers.

Thus, peopled purely with believers, the kingdom will do well and survive a long time. John reveals in Revelation 20 that the kingdom will endure a thousand years, and hence it is called the Millennium (*mille*-thousand; *annum*-year).

PEACE ON EARTH

As King, Jesus achieves what no other ruler has accomplished—peace. For one thousand years the world will experience no war at all.

The Antichrist, with his supernatural powers and huge armies, maintains world peace for a brief period between the Russian invasion of Israel and the Armageddon, but it is the cold war peace we are all familiar with.

Jesus brings the peace foreseen by Isaiah:

> And they will hammer their swords into plowshares, and their spears into pruning hooks. Nation will not lift up sword against nation, and never again will they learn war. (Isaiah 2:4)

The United Nations building in New York City bears a portion of this Scripture on its entrance, but unfortunately it is quoted without the full context. Missing is the first statement of Isaiah 2:4, "And He will judge between the nations." God has been left out, as usual. It is not until the Lord makes His judgments among the nations that the kingdom and its full-time peace will prevail.

How ironic for the world's most celebrated peacemakers to quote from a Book that contains the solutions to all of their problems but fail to read the whole Book, or even the whole Scripture that they find suitable.

This world has at least a five-thousand-year history of war with no indications that it will ever be otherwise. Even today, modern man, conqueror of so much disease,

"THY KINGDOM COME...IN EARTH, AS IT IS IN HEAVEN"

tamer of nature, and explorer of space, still spends most of his time and money fighting. "Defense" claims the riches of every modern nation in proportion to its size, and man's ultimate scientific know-how goes into killing (or, a new term adjusted to our times, overkilling).

The Bible analyzes the problem as a basic maladjustment of men to their Creator and thus to one another. Jesus said, "Peace I leave with you" (John 14:27), and those in relationship to Him know the deepest meaning of that promise. But it will take His very reappearance to accomplish that over the whole of the earth, and then only when the unbelievers have almost killed off their kind.

But Isaiah's fondest visions of peace will be achieved when the Lord returns. Isaiah sees enthusiastic, spiritually motivated people of the world going up to Jerusalem in the Millennium and taking an interest in government:

> Now it will come about that in the last days, the mountain of the house of the LORD will be established as the chief of the mountains [at the Jerusalem Temple site¹], and will be raised above the hills; and all the nations will stream to it. And many peoples will come and say, "Come, let us go up to the mountain of the LORD, to the house of the God of Jacob; that He may teach us concerning His ways, and that we may walk in His paths." For the law will go forth from Zion [Israel], and the word of the LORD from Jerusalem. (2:2-3)

Worthy subjects of a worthy king! Those will be the days!

This remarkable change in world affairs will affect even the animals. They will all become peace-lovers. Isaiah says,

> And the wolf will dwell with the lamb, and the leopard will lie down with the kid, and the calf and the young

lion and the fatling together; and a little boy will lead them. . . . The lion will eat straw like the ox. (11:6-7)

The animals will live together and eat from the fields instead of killing each other as man has done. Even a little child need have no fear of wild animals in the peaceful times to come.

It will be a changed world in more ways than that. No one will die in the Millennium, but children will be born. At first the population will be a little smaller than we are used to, but it will include, along with those we have specified, all the faithful Christians of the church age and the saved Old Testament believers. They will all be resurrected, like their King, and outfitted for immortality.

World history will be a strange subject, if it is discussed at all. It will be exceedingly difficult to convince the children that come along in the happy Millennium that men once hated and killed one another. But the information will be available—particularly in the Bible, which, as we have seen, will be a steady topic of discussion in government circles. The Bible chronicles man's old way of doing things, and Jesus observed that heaven and earth would pass away before this best-seller would go out of print. "The earth will be full of the knowledge of the LORD as the waters cover the sea," says Isaiah (11:9).

The twelve apostles will rule over the twelve tribes of Israel, as it enjoys true favored-nation status, and all of those who were "faithful in a very little" (Luke 19:17) will be given great responsibilities under the new regime.

No wonder the Lord urged His followers to pray, "Thy kingdom come!"

WATCH OUT, EGYPT!

The Millennium sounds like a perfect world, but in some small ways it will not be. Amazingly enough, men

151

will still insist on their rebellious ways, though to quite a lesser degree, even in that ultimate earthly utopia.

The fault lies deeply within the nature of men—in the sin nature they inherited from their common father, Adam. The men born during the Millennium will have the same fatal flaw, and though they will maintain a peaceful world alongside the many believers, some tests of obedience will still be necessary.

Zechariah supplies that the feast of Tabernacles, commemorating the deliverance of the Hebrew nation from slavery in Egypt to their Promised Land, will still be celebrated each year. And attendance will be mandatory.

> Then it will come about that any who are left of all the nations that went against Jerusalem will go up from year to year to worship the King, the LORD of hosts, and to celebrate the Feast of Booths. And it will be that whichever of the families of the earth does not go up to Jerusalem to worship the King, the LORD of hosts, there will be no rain on them. (Zechariah 14:16-17)

And, as if the Lord knows full well just *who* among the family of nations might fail to appear for the grand old Jewish feast, He says,

> And if the family of Egypt does not go not up or enter, then no rain will fall on them; it will be the plague with which the LORD smites the nations who do not go up to celebrate the Feast of Booths. (v. 18, italics added)

And yet again, as if a word to the wise were not going to be sufficient, He warns,

> This will be the punishment of Egypt, and the punishment of all the nations who do not go up to celebrate the Feast of Booths. (v. 19, italics added)

If Israel has ever had a dependable enemy it is Egypt, and somehow it appears than even in the Millennium the Egyptians will be loath to offer this simple allegiance to the Lord. Perhaps the Scripture singles out Egypt for emphasis; that is, if Egypt is required to attend, then certainly all the other nations are. We'll have to wait and see.

It makes a peculiar picture. There will be "heathen" in the Millennium as it progresses. Men have always been free, and they will apparently continue to be free to choose God or not. But they will have to render this specified allegiance to Christ once each year. That's hardly as much allegiance as men now pay their respective unbelieving governments. But if they refuse even this small token, they will have some troubles. It's hard to plant when there's no rain—particularly in places like Egypt.

As the centuries pass in the Millennium, and as the population grows, a certain rebellious spirit will foment among the nations. Of course it does not come to war during the Millennium, but at its very end there is something of a replay of the Russian invasion of Israel.

Satan has not been done away with but has been bound helpless for the thousand-year period. At the end of the Millennium he is released for one last try (in effect) at corrupting the world. And he finds armies available.

This final battle is given little space in the Scriptures. John's Revelation covers it in a few verses (20:7-10). Satan is defeated quickly and this time banished to the eternal lake of fire, never to rise up again.

ON TO ETERNITY

We can't say much about eternity, because it is a totally supernatural phenomenon. At the end of the Millennium, our story of the coming Russian invasion of Israel is finished; its steady chain of events is finally ended.

The world will undergo a change unlike anything since creation.

God will revamp everything. There will be a new heaven, a new earth, and a new Jerusalem. There will be no more time. The oceans will disappear. John reports an incredible scene:

> And I saw a new heaven and a new earth; for the first heaven and the first earth passed away, and there was no longer any sea. And I saw the holy city, new Jerusalem, coming down out of heaven from God, made ready as a bride adorned for her husband. (Revelation 21:1-2)

What kind of picture does that make? Where was John standing? What does a city coming down from the sky look like? Where did the first heaven and the first earth go?

Obviously, those are matters much beyond the scope of today's observer. Perhaps those in the Millennium, who have lived a thousand years and have seen Christ on the earth, will be able to confront such mysteries. There is not space in this little book about war to discuss eternity.

Believers will be there, of course; but heaven only knows (literally!) what form we'll take. We can't live without water, and rain will be needed even in the Millennium, but in eternity there will be a new earth with no seas. We look up at the sky now and think of it as heaven, but that sky is going away somewhere, and a new one will be installed. What is under our feet—the earth—will be something utterly new.

Another judgment will be held for entrance into eternity. That is the famed Judgment Day when Christ will open the book of life and will judge every unbelieving soul who ever walked this earth. The sea will give up her dead, and even hell will be opened to deliver up its dead (Revelation 20:12-13). The billions of souls who inhabited the eons of earthly time will be judged "according to their deeds" one by one!

"And if anyone's name was not found written in the book of life," concludes John, "he was thrown into the lake of fire" (20:15).

NOTE

1. See Thomas McCall and Zola Levitt, *Satan in the Sanctuary* (Chicago: Moody, 1973).

13

"False Prophets Will Abound": Facts vs. Rumors

THE NEED FOR AN ENLIGHTENED VIEW OF PROPHECY

The last three decades or so have brought a new interest in end-times prophecy. People who had not previously given a thought to the second coming were inspired by the 1967 Six-Day War as Israel confirmed its role as a viable member of the family of modern nations and recaptured Jerusalem, with its revered Temple Mount. The Yom Kippur War in 1973 had a similar consciousness-raising effect as Israel survived its severest test. In the ensuing period, the Soviet Union became a dominant force in the Middle East and the European economic conglomerate raised the specter of a united Europe reminiscent of the old Roman Empire.

With the Iraqi invasion of Kuwait and the accompanying events in Israel, Saudi Arabia, Russia, and the United States, and at the United Nations, there was much discussion among believers about topics such as Armageddon, the future of Israel and Babylon, and the second coming of the Lord. It seems it takes a war in the Middle East to really generate sustained interest in the end of the age among the general public, or even among evangelical Christians.

But along with a spiritually healthy interest in Bible prophecy there has developed an undercurrent of what we believe is a negative interest in the field of eschatology (study of last things). We who believe the Word of God should not be led astray with "every wind of doctrine" that blows our way, Scripture admonishes. On the contrary, we need to develop an enlightened view of prophecy that hones in on what is factual and vital and ignores those things that are not doctrinally sound, are inconsequential, or are based more on rumor than on fact. Our Lord taught vigorously about His second coming, but He warned just as strongly against following after the false Christs and false prophets who would attend the end of the age (Matthew 24:5, 11).

The "Gift of Prophecy": "Confirmation by the Lord"

There are those who claim to have the gift of prophecy and endeavor to predict events of which the Scriptures say nothing at all. Such persons range from astrologers and soothsayers, who consult all kinds of entities to come up with their prognostications, to professing Christian preachers who announce over radio and television their ability to foresee the future. They cite various "confirmations" by the Lord, identifying themselves as prophets and their message as authentic prophecy. It is our conviction that the gift of prophecy ceased with the gift of apostleship and that anyone who claims to be able to prophesy is violating the warning at the end of the book of Revelation against adding to the "words of the prophecy of this book": they will add to themselves the plagues described in that same book (Revelation 22:18).

We are not prophets, nor do we have the gift of prophecy. If we have any gift from the Lord it is to expound what He has already revealed in the Word through His true prophets, including Christ Himself, Moses, Isaiah, Ezekiel, and Daniel, as well as the apostles. We can and do strive to take what God has revealed to us in His Word, treat it with respect and due diligence, seek illumination from the Holy Spirit, and attempt to come up with a reasonable interpretation of the "whole counsel of God." We therefore applaud those who have endeavored to do the difficult but always exciting work of interpretation, and we are more than skeptical of those who claim powers that are not scripturally permissible for them to claim, no matter how alluring their concepts may be.

SOME UNSUBSTANTIATED RUMORS

Throughout the past few decades, although interest in prophetic matters has accelerated, there have been many significant and authentic signs that the return of the Lord may be near indeed. Those include the restoration of Israel to the land, the apostasy within the church, and the rise of Russia and a united Europe as leading players on the world stage. But there have also been some unsubstantiated rumors with great bearing on prophecy that have spread like wildfire among evangelical Christians. When one looks more closely at those rumors they typically evaporate into nothing much and they appear to be hoaxes perpetrated by religious hucksters on the uninformed and gullible. Oftentimes rumors are passed on through otherwise respectable newsletters with little or no investigation or qualification, and readers are left with the impression that these are verified facts. Those who pass on stories in such a fashion are unworthy journalists who can actually do harm to the cause of legitimate biblical interpretation.

Below is a short list of some of the more popular yarns that have traveled from church to church and village to village, distracting Christians almost everywhere.

Stones for the Temple. One of the most persistent rumors of our time was that actual stones for the rebuilding of the Temple in Jerusalem were cut and stored for shipment in the excellent limestone quarries of Indiana. The story was reported not long after the Six-Day War, when Israel's recapture of the Temple Mount inspired believers at a time when the idea of the rebuilding of the Temple was on many people's minds. Somehow the theory of American limestone for the Temple ran rampant throughout the evangelical Christian world and was repeated in newsletters, on the radio and television, and from pulpits, usually as fact, with little or no qualification. Finally, some investigators, including Zola Levitt, asked some questions around the major Indiana quarries, including the often-cited one at Bedford, and no one of consequence knew anything about such an order of stones for the Temple. The rumor was thoroughly repudiated, but every once in a while one still hears echoes of that wishful thinking, decades later.

Unfortunately, with the repudiation of the rumor there came a general view that the prophecy in the Scriptures concerning the rebuilding of the Temple was also repudiated. That, of course, is not the case, but it demonstrates one of the difficulties Bible students face as we endeavor to separate wheat from chaff and truth from rumor.

Vultures laying four eggs. In Revelation 19 John beholds the spectacle of the angel of the Lord preparing the world for Armageddon: "And I saw an angel standing in the sun; and he cried with a loud voice, saying to all the birds which fly in midheaven, 'Come, assemble for the great supper of God; in order that you may eat the flesh of kings'" (vv. 17-18a).

Apparently, some claimed, the carrion will be so prodigious at the conclusion of Armageddon that it will take far more than all the birds of prey now available to devour the flesh of the dead invaders. And so a rumor developed that the vulture population in the Middle East was increasing exponentially. The birds in the area were laying four eggs at a time instead of the customary one or, at most, two. Birds of prey were becoming so numerous, according to the story, that they were soon going to be a general nuisance. Again the yarn raced around the world on the wings of some secular, but mostly Christian, news media, with scarcely any investigation and practically no disclaimers. It was repeated over and over as literal fact, and those who communicated the story were convinced that God was multiplying the vulture population in order to fulfill that prophecy.

But if there was any increase in the vulture population it was apparently short-lived. No one is talking about vulture eggs anymore, and evidently that was just another unsubstantiated rumor. John's prophecy does relate that all the birds of prey in the area are going to be called to the great feast on the dead bodies of the enemies of the Lord, but there is no indication that the Lord will create an extra supply of vultures for the purpose. Again, less than rigorous journalism and sensationalist teaching mar and obscure a great truth of biblical prophecy.

The *"Beast"* computer. The high tech world has not escaped the rumor mill either. The Antichrist is portrayed in prophecy as having control of the economic levers of the world, so that no one will be allowed to even buy or sell without "the mark of the beast," the identifying number everyone will have during the Tribulation. How will the Antichrist be able to control everyone so directly and in such detail, especially considering the very human propensity for delving into the black market when supplies get tight? It has been suggested that by harnessing the power of the modern supercomputers the Antichrist could control the economy of the entire world and all its people. And, a few years ago, such a computer suddenly appeared on the scene, at least in rumor. Word got out that somewhere in Western Europe there was already a gigantic mainframe computer so powerful it could track billions of people and their individual economic activities. It was of such universal capability and so potentially malevolent that it was nicknamed "The Beast." (Or perhaps the title was affectionately given by the intimidated programmers of some such machine.)

Such was the story that emanated from newsletters, pulpits, and media. There was already in place a tool that could be utilized by the Antichrist in his political and economic conquest of the world. But, as in the other cases, the rumor did not stand up to the test of rigorous investigation. "The Beast" apparently was another figment of someone's fertile and overactive imagination.

"Down with Christian broadcasting!" The next rumor did not have quite so much to do with prophecy, as it concerned the present proclamation of the gospel and the truth of the Word (but see Matthew 24:14). It was overheard that Madalyn Murray O'Hair was out to eliminate Christian radio and television programs from the airwaves. Inspired by the cranky atheist, the Federal Communications Commission was going to bar such programming, some people supposed. Documents were produced showing the nefarious plan, and a letter-writing campaign targeting the FCC and Congress was launched, urging that the plan to destroy Christian programming be stopped. Many congressmen and various federal agencies denied that any such plan was in the works, but the more it was denied the more shrill and emotional was the outcry. Christian broadcasters were exasperated to have to urge their supporters to cool off their unwarranted attacks on the government. There simply never was any

such threat, but to this day, some fifteen years down the line, the FCC still receives letters on the subject.

We suppose it is comforting to know that there are those who would come to the defense of the proclamation of the gospel on the airways if it really were threatened, but again, what kind of credibility are we developing with such hypersensitive behavior?

Social Security cards with the "666" code number. Someone created the notion that the government had started to issue Social Security cards with the code number "666" on them (right out of Revelation—"the mark of the Beast"). There was no truth whatsoever to that theory, but during the late 70s and the early 80s every second or third question on Zola Levitt's radio talk show concerned that rumor. Levitt finally traced the rumor to its supposed source, a minor official in another state, and telephoned that person on the air. The man could supply no information whatever about the story and had no idea how it got started.

Finding the arks: Part I, Part II. The Ark of the Covenant, that singular sacred artifact of Judaism that once graced the Holy of Holies in the Tabernacle and later in the first Temple of God in Jerusalem, has sparked popular and distracting prophecy fulfillment rumors. There are folks who say it was buried in the mount under the Temple and that the powers that be in Jerusalem really know where it is, and others say it is in Jordan or Ethiopia. The Ark is never really found, but the story never really dies either.

In 1990, Zola Levitt interviewed the author of a bestselling book concerning the Ethiopian theory. One had to believe that the Queen of Sheba had married King Solomon and that their offspring had arranged (some four centuries later) to spirit the Ark out of Jerusalem to Ethiopia when the siege of Nebuchadnezzar occurred in 586 B.C. One also had to believe that that family continued in an unbroken line from that time through some twenty-five centuries and always kept the secret of the location of the Ark in Ethiopia. One finally had to believe that that author was privy to that secret of two and one-half millennia and that for a proper royalty contract he could be persuaded to reveal it to hundreds of millions of Americans. Similar rumors of the Ark's discovery have followed through the years, all unsubstantiated.

Closely following the adventures of the Ark of the Covenant are those concerning Noah's ark. In this case, the location is clearly seen in Scripture (Mount Ararat), and if we have identified the correct mountain we can theoretically, at least, climb that mountain and take a look. But as with the finding of the Ark of the Covenant, we have interviewed several Noah's ark researchers and some who have climbed Mount Ararat. Unfortunately, their enthusiastic testimonials to sightings of "dark objects" or "tooled wood" were not substantiated with pictures or reasonable facsimiles of a boat or a part of a boat. So in this case also, although the object being sought is real and important, the evidence for its discovery is simply too speculative to rely on.

Ashes of the red heifer. Many students of biblical prophecy agree with us about the necessity of the Temple's being rebuilt in Jerusalem in the last days; however, some believe the event requires the discovery of the actual ashes of the ancient altar of the Temple in order to continue the flame of the consecrated Temple altar. Proponents of that assumption are of the opinion that the remains of that ancient fire are necessary because they contain the ashes of the red heifer that was consecrated by Moses and Aaron and passed down from generation to generation during the time of the first and second Temples. It is their persuasion that the ashes were carefully hidden during the destruction of the Second Temple by the Romans in A.D. 70 and that they must now be rediscovered in order to have a properly sanctified altar fire. At any rate, there are those who are actively seeking the ashes of the red heifer in Israel, and some who actually claim to have found the mysterious substance. (Others seek a perfect red heifer in order to create new ashes, but that is another story.)

Our conviction is that such a discovery may not be necessary to the reinstatement of worship in the Temple. There is no mention in the Scriptures that the fire of the first Temple was preserved intact for use in the second Temple when it was built after the Babylonian captivity (although there is some indication of that in the Apocrypha). And no Scripture or nonbiblical passage states that even the sacred Ark of the Covenant itself was used in the second Temple. That most holy artifact of Judaism had simply disappeared. It would seem that if any element of the ancient Temple were necessary for its reinstatement it would certainly be the Ark of the Covenant. But if even the Ark were not required for the second Temple, why should the relatively less sacred ashes of the red heifer be necessary for the third Temple?

Zola Levitt was able to interview an orthodox Jewish scholar who was close to the source of that particular notion. Associated with the Jerusalem Great Synagogue, he was present the day members of the Orthodox community declared that the ashes had been found. In reality, thought that observer, it was not a real find but rather an attempt to stop some archeology at the site of the Temple Mount. There has long been a controversy between those who wish to honor Israel by keeping up its ancient traditions, including those of not disturbing burial grounds, historical artifacts, and so forth, and those who wish to honor Israel by digging up its past, whether or not they disturb some artifacts. In that case, a "find" of such magnitude instantly stopped the picks and shovels of the archaeologists, and the Orthodox had their way.

The veracity of the find of the ashes, however, raised much skepticism. In the view of the scholarly commentator, definitely a supporter of the Orthodox side of the argument, the ashes really were never found.

But there was perhaps no story that traveled farther in American churches in the latter half of the twentieth century than this one. During the height of Christian interest in this report, speakers on prophetic subjects sometimes were unable to conduct an orderly question and answer period after a speaking engagement because every single question concerned this highly suspect find.

What are we to make of all those rumors, which seem to fit into the prophetic scheme but turn out to be unfounded? They end up hurting the cause of serious study of biblical prophecy, of course. False alarms are seldom helpful in forecasting real emergencies.

It would seem that evangelical Christians should have some reasonable standards of verification before repeating hearsay, however fascinating it may be to those inclined toward studying prophecy. If we must pass on a rumor, either through teaching, preaching, or the various avenues of the media, we should specify that it is nothing more than an unconfirmed rumor. We should also do what we can to research the matter. In that way, perhaps we can help maintain credibility in the evangelical Christian media and in the all-important mission of proclaiming the coming of the Lord.

14

A Strategy for Christians

Why is God telling us about future events?

Did prophecy ever save anybody? Will the fact that Christians quote the Bible about the future impress unbelievers?

Perhaps, but cases in the Bible itself show otherwise. When Jeremiah shouted that the Babylonians were going to destroy Jerusalem and the mighty Temple of God, he was jailed for annoying the government. When Jesus, looking sadly at the great second Temple, said, "Not one stone here shall be left upon another" (Matthew 24:2), He was ridiculed.

Yet, God chose to reveal His plans in advance to those who would read them. What is His purpose? What are we supposed to do?

This chapter is for Christians—those who believe in Jesus and His atoning work. The next chapter is for the unbelievers—practical suggestions for hard times ahead.

We put this one first because the rapture might come before you finish this book.

We can suggest two reasons that God has chosen to reveal the future. One is timing. As we follow events as they happen, we get a sense of just where we are in God's scheme of things. The other reason is so that we know the alternative to belief in Christ. That alternative is so horrible that it might well spur us on to greater efforts to reach this world for Christ.

This is a late hour for reaching the world, but remember the thief on the cross. He had mere hours to live, but we'll see him in the kingdom!

Christians can relax, if we wish. The rapture will take us off this sinking ship, and we'll be spared further grief. But in the good example of the One who laid down His very life for His friends, we can do better than that.

The apostle gave a word of advice for these times:

> And let us consider how to stimulate one another to love and good deeds, not forsaking our own assembling together, as is the habit of some, but encouraging one another; and all the more, as you see the day drawing near. (Hebrews 10:24-25)

The "day approaching" is the Lord's day—the day when He will commence judging. That day is the fulfillment of prophecy. "So much the more" should we heed this advice as that day approaches.

We are in a much better position than those at the time of the apostles to see that day approaching when it will be too late to help this world. We have our prophecy —our time schedule, as it were. We can check off events as they happen.

When we started to write this book, there was no Yom Kippur War as yet. There was no really reasonable thought of a Russian invasion of Israel in the offing. It would have shocked the world if Russia had invaded Israel at that time.

But a few months later, Russia did shock the world by reportedly mobilizing troops for that war!

We almost ticked off another event in just a few months. May God help us to get this prophecy book to you before it becomes a history book!

Back to the apostle's good advice. Believers are urged not to avoid gathering together and to exhort one another in spiritual graces and good works. We are not to be spiritual hermits, exulting in the fact that our Lord is going to get us out of all this; we are rather to become actively involved with other believers in the wonderful thing that is faith in God.

The effect will be obvious. If believers can show the world a united, triumphant front in these troubled times, it may cause some of the world to think. They may want to know why we are as we are, and we surely can tell them.

Our churches, our media, and all of our people—Christ's people—need to be stirred up to realize that our Lord gave us a great commission. We are to share the gospel; we are to preach "to every creature" (Mark 16:15, KJV).

When John had finished seeing his incredible revelation of the future, with all its stupefying scenes of the last days of this whole creation, he began to witness. In his brief and beautiful way he said,

> And the Spirit and the bride say, "Come." And let the one who hears say, "Come." And let the one who is thirsty come; let the one who wishes take the water of life without cost. (Revelation 22:17)

How fitting a statement: Let him take the water of life freely! In the Millennium, the unbeliever who will not approach the Lord will have no rain. In eternity there is no sea. We have all the water that's left!

If knowing prophecy does not move us to share our faith, something is very wrong. To understand the condition and destiny of literally billions of unsaved people who are plunging headlong toward horrible lives and horrible deaths, to realize through prophecy that the very politics of today's world are rapidly bringing this to pass, to know in addition that a solution to all of this coming agony is readily available to all—to know all that is to be put in a position of most solemn responsibility.

If we know all that and still fail to tell the world at every chance, then we are acting in an unchristian way.

HERE COMES THE BRIDE

The Bride of Christ, the church, the body of believers, is this world's only chance. We must not fail in this. Our God is "not wishing for any to perish" (2 Peter 3:9), and He commissioned us to do the hard work of reaching the lost. The Spirit and the Bride say, "Come."

When we say, "Come," we are extending quite an invitation. We are admitting our friends to the rapture, to the very wedding of Jesus Christ, to the millennial kingdom, and to everlasting life in eternity. And think what we are getting them out of!

When our friends accept our invitation to those coming spectacular events, they inherit all of our heaven-sent assurances immediately. And we who are believers today have the profoundly relieving assurance that we will not have to go through the Tribulation period on earth. The rapture will come before that!

It is not entirely clear whether we will see the coming Russian invasion of Israel, however. We have placed it just at the beginning of the Tribulation period—perhaps preceding it slightly. We have stated that there are widely differing opinions on this, and that the rapture

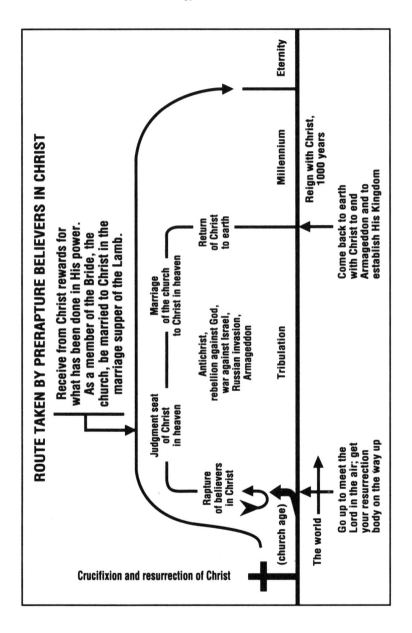

ROUTE TAKEN BY PRERAPTURE BELIEVERS IN CHRIST

Receive from Christ rewards for what has been done in His power. As a member of the Bride, the church, be married to Christ in the marriage supper of the Lamb.

Marriage of the church to Christ in heaven

Judgment seat of Christ in heaven

Antichrist, rebellion against God, war against Israel, Russian invasion, Armageddon

Rapture of believers in Christ

Return of Christ to earth

Tribulation

Millennium

Eternity

Reign with Christ, 1000 years

Come back to earth with Christ to end Armageddon and to establish His Kingdom

(church age)

The world →

Go up to meet the Lord in the air; get your resurrection body on the way up

Crucifixion and resurrection of Christ

might occur at any moment. It is good to remember that nothing in prophecy has to happen before the rapture.

The events of Ezekiel 36 and 37 have happened before our eyes. We have seen the "dry bones"—the Jewish people scattered in the "graveyards" of the Gentile nations—regathered to the Promised Land. We have seen a nation form there and maintain itself for close to a half-century. Ezekiel goes on with the Russian invasion of Israel immediately in his next chapters, 38 and 39, noting nothing to happen in between.

It is conjecture to assume that that means we will see the invasion, but we have the advantage over past analysts in that we live in times of evident fulfillment of prophecy. From a purely worldly standpoint, it would surprise no one if Russia invaded Israel in the very near future.

The surprises would come in the results of that invasion.

Also, we might say that the point of the rapture is to spare believers the real holocaust to come. The Russian invasion of Israel is a confined war, by the prophet's description. It would likely have little effect on the church, which is not found in great numbers in either Russia or the Middle East. The world has weathered the Yom Kippur War with its dreary outcome and presumably could put up with that one, too, without undue damage.

Then again, there is the supernatural factor to consider. Logically, God would hold off the rapture as long as possible in order to gather as many souls to the harvest as He can. But He acts in a visible way in the Russian invasion. We have seen that fire comes down on the Russian armies, and unless that description relates to nuclear attack or something we can understand in an earthly way, God would be "exposing" Himself to the world.

It is held by many commentators that when God actually shows Himself by His actions, the age of faith is over.

In any case, we hold that the rapture and the Russian invasion of Israel are close together, near the beginning of the Tribulation period. If we are right in that, signs of the Russian invasion are virtually signs of the rapture.

During that scary Yom Kippur week when the Russians reportedly were mobilizing troops, we seemed to be very close to fulfilling end-times prophecy. That a situation very like that seen by Ezekiel could happen in these times certainly suggests that the fulfillment of his visions is quite possible—and maybe very close.

So, in a way, we are rapidly becoming friends in need to our unbelieving fellow men. It's no longer a question of "Come to our church," but more like "Avoid the Antichrist and Armageddon."

Our knowledge, which the Lord has imparted to us, is of inestimable value to the world. If we withhold it, we would be like researchers withholding a cure for cancer. We have the truth, and as our Lord said, "The truth shall make you free" (John 8:32).

We can calculate the timing of God's plan by watching our world. We can see the alternatives to going with God by just reading the prophecy in the Bible.

The strategy for Christians has been disclosed:

> And Jesus came up and spoke to them, saying, "All authority has been given to Me in heaven and on earth. Go therefore and make disciples of all the nations, baptizing them in the name of the Father and the Son and the Holy Spirit, teaching them to observe all that I commanded you; and lo, I am with you always, even to the end of the age." (Matthew 28:18-20)

15

A Strategy for Unbelievers

Perhaps, however, you do not believe in Christ, and we have not persuaded you. Perhaps you have found this book to be good bedtime reading and an entertaining theory of things to come, but you figure you'll make out on your own wits as you always have.

Very well. First, please know that we love you.

We don't mean to sound fatuous, but we'd hardly be good representatives of Jesus Christ on earth if we failed to love all men as He commanded. But it is not just a matter of following His dictum. We are *able* to love you. Christianity has the peculiar effect of imbuing the plainest individuals with a real ability to love—even to love enemies, as our Lord also counseled. We do not regard you as an enemy, but rather a brother—a brother in great need.

So, if you will, we would like to make a few suggestions about the future. In view of all of the coming circumstances we have outlined, we think you should take action.

First of all, the Bible itself gives one imperative to unbelievers. "Believe on the Lord Jesus Christ, and you shall be saved" (Acts 16:31). We would be remiss to leave that out. We think it's still the only way to go.

Failing that, let's consider reasonable alternatives. Since the coming Russian invasion of Israel appears to be in preparation these days, and since that seems to start the whole chain of tragic events associated with the end times, you'd better get moving!

Discussing the effects of the abortive Russian invasion, Ezekiel specifies that there will be fire on Magog and among those who dwell securely in the coastlands (see 39:6). This cryptic "coastlands" is more easily understood when we look at it in the context of Ezekiel's world. In that Mediterranean area, most countries were more densely settled along their coasts to facilitate trade. Ships were the ultimate tool of international commerce. The present United States is still an example of more densely settled coastlands than inland areas. Ezekiel's term indicated the civilizations across the seas from Israel.

It is possible, then, that we Americans are counted among those "who inhabit the coastlands in safety" and that this "fire" capable of wiping out the enormous allied forces of the Russian invasion will have its effects elsewhere. That view is especially reasonable when we consider the overwhelming destruction of nuclear warfare and its resulting fallout.

Therefore, it would be good if you would now install a bomb shelter capable of resisting atomic-scale warfare and radiation. People may think you're a bit paranoid, but they also laughed at Noah until it started to rain.

Fortunately, although the destruction resulting from the Russian invasion appears to be very widespread, it's over quickly, and the world goes on. Let us assume you have taken our advice about the bomb shelter and have survived. What next?

Next you should watch for the rapture of the church. That will be unmistakable. The Christians will simply disappear. Since they are to meet the Lord in the air, they will just be "gone" all at once. There has been a lot of conjecture about how that will happen and how it will be explained, but remember, we are dealing here with a period of divine activity, and lots of things are going to seem strange.

Conceivably, those two events—the invasion and the rapture—will be in the other order, as we have explained, but in any case, they'll be close together.

The one or the other may make a believer out of you. Jonah, who resisted the Lord's directives, had a definite change of heart when he came back out of the great fish! But assuming that your faith in godlessness still persists, you are in for the long ride. Once the rapture has occurred, your chance to be airlifted out of all this is over. You can always still turn to Christ, but you'll have your troubles!

The next thing to watch for is the appearance of the Antichrist. That will occur right after the rapture and, we think, right after the Russian invasion.

If you are a typical unbeliever of that day, you will say to the Antichrist, "Thank you. At last we're going to have peace"; and you will bow down to that glib egomaniac like all the others. You will note with distaste a continuing Christian activity, but you will be delighted to participate in the new regime of the Tribulation period. You'll gladly have your number tattooed on your skin so that you can go shopping conveniently; and you'll think the world has at last pulled itself together.

Memories of this book and many others that warned about such things may come to your mind from time to time, but you'll think, *Those fellows had no appreciation for what men can accomplish when they get together.*

The joke is on you!

You'll sigh with gladness over the peace in the Middle East, and you'll watch the Tribulation Temple, a truly magnificent piece of architecture, rise in Jerusalem. You will probably think, *You have to give those Jews credit. They really hang in there. When the going gets tough, the tough get going.* (The Temple might be actually constructed ahead of the other events, but, in any case, it will be standing and functioning by the middle of the Tribulation period.)

You'll watch with approval, if you are a typical unbeliever, as the Antichrist signs a treaty with Israel; and it will seem to you that the troublesome powder keg will at last be permanently defused.

But getting back to our suggestions for you, that treaty-signing will start your last seven years, and you should act accordingly. It might be best to sell everything you have and get really far away from the Middle East. You're on your way to Armageddon.

You may chance across a witness for Christ at this late date. He may be one of those 144,000 preachers of Israel, and you may find him appealing on account of his very stubbornness and courage under fire.

May we recommend him to you? It still won't be too late. He'll provide you safe passage to the Millennium if you'll believe.

But you may resist him because belief in Christ will be a very risky proposition at that point. The Antichrist will have everybody computerized, and the remaining Christians will be on the most stupendous "enemies list" of all time. You may want to avoid that. You'll see Christians actually executed for their faith.

Frankly, we would encourage you to take this life-and-death risk. If you come to believe in the Lord Jesus, you will pass into the new kingdom. If you do not, sooner or later you will die forever. To resist out of fear would be to trade eternity for less than seven years of the worst possible earthly life. In this particular case, you are truly worth more dead than alive.

But at least be kind to that Hebrew Christian preacher. Remember, Jesus will take that behavior into consideration in the immigration office of the Millennium. If you have the chance to feed a starving Jew, or to clothe him, or to comfort him while he is sick or in prison, for your own sake do so! Become a sheep and be separated from the goats!

Eventually you will see the Antichrist go into the new Jerusalem Temple and proclaim himself God. That may strike you as a bit egotistical, but we have tolerated such excesses in our leaders before. You'll probably go along with it.

At all costs, resist having the identifying number stamped on you, if it has not been done already. You may go hungry for a while because you will not be able to go through the checkout line at the local supermarket without your number, but you'll be better off foraging for food than being judged later on. It's not quite clear when that particular legislation will take place, but even under the Antichrist's computerized systems, it will take some time to number everybody in the world. You may have a chance to hold off. By all means, do so!

But if you go along with this too, your alternatives have really run out. Assuming that you bear the Antichrist's number, have not taken the opportunity to be kind to the brethren of the Lord, and still do not believe in Jesus Christ, everything else will be done *for* you.

If you have never had the opportunity to visit Israel, you will go at government expense when you are drafted into the Antichrist's army. If you can, you should seek high ground in Israel because of virtual seas of blood as high as the bridles of the horses. If you can make yourself

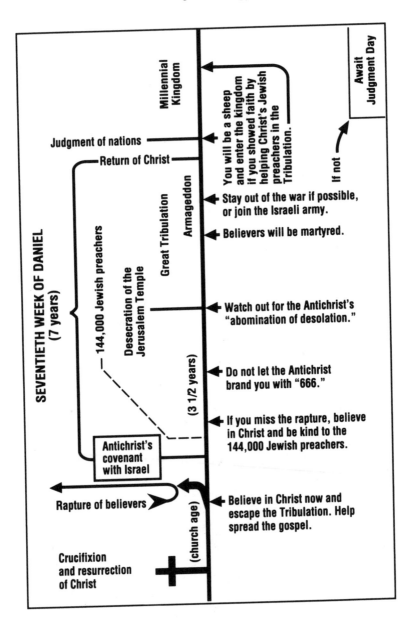

scarce enough to survive the demolishing of the Gentile forces by Jesus and His heavenly army, you will make it as far as the trial before the throne of Christ. But you will be a goat, and the verdict will be "eternal punishment" (Matthew 25:46).

We are not threatening you. We're just quoting the Book that contains all the rest of our information. We've seen too much of it come true to doubt it at this point.

We don't know precisely what that everlasting punishment will be, but we know about the alternative. Bear with us a little longer, while we explain.

A More Excellent Way

To quote a phrase from Scripture, "Behold, I show you a more excellent way."

Anything would be "more excellent" than the way the Bible says things are going to be for unbelievers. The alternative to the end-times holocaust is so pleasant and so simply attained that we feel we must say it one last time, complete with the method.

Believers, as we have seen, will see the rapture, the Millennium, and eternity, rather than destruction and punishment. You can become a believer virtually at once.

The Lord's attitude on your salvation is clear: "I stand at the door and knock" (Revelation 3:20). He is "not wishing for any to perish" (2 Peter 3:9). "But as many as received Him, to them He gave the right to become children of God" (John 1:12).

Approaching God is quite a natural thing. He is, after all, the Creator of nature. There is hardly a thinking person anywhere who cannot see that nature has a Maker and that the affairs of this world give the impression of having a plan. Supplied further with the truths of prophecy and the fact that they are coming to pass, the unbeliever can readily approach God without feeling strange.

You do not have to write or phone. God has indicated that He will hear you whatever your circumstances, wherever you are.

You do not have to be anybody special. Jesus had time for the lepers and thieves as well as for the mighty and powerful. You do not have to qualify in any special social group; the tax collectors and prostitutes go into heaven before the befrocked high priests of Israel, according to Jesus.

You do not have to change yourself; God delights in taking care of that in return for your faith. You will be a happier, kinder, more loving individual, as you have always wanted to be, when Christ takes over your life.

And you will get the world's best "buyer protection plan." You will live on and on in joy and peace, avoiding the terrible ending of this world as we know it and proceeding to the best of all possible worlds. In talking to God, use your own words. He knows you, and there's no use putting up a false front.

You might try saying something on this order:

Lord Jesus, I believe that You died for me and can give me everlasting life. Please do this for me and let me live for You from now on. Thanks.

Do it now. And we'll see you in the kingdom!

16

"No Man Knows": The Day or the Hour

DATE SETTING: SCRIPTURALLY PROHIBITED

Many things are certain in Christianity. The apostle John wrote his first epistle to assure us that we could know for certain that we who have trusted in Christ have eternal life, forgiveness of sins, and a loving Father who has provided us with the clear gospel record of the death, burial, and resurrection of our Lord. If Scripture is believed, there is no ambiguity about this marvelous array of truths.

But other parts of Scripture have more uncertainty attached to them. An issue that definitely is not spelled out in the Word is the time of the return of Christ. The fact of His return is definite, but the timing of the event is left entirely uncertain. "And so when they had come together, they were asking Him, saying, 'Lord, is it at this time You are restoring the kingdom to Israel?' He said to them, 'It is not for you to know times or epochs which the Father has fixed by His own authority'" (Acts 1:6-7).

Nevertheless, a perennial theme among some Christian writers, especially those who teach biblical prophecy, is speculation about the date of the rapture of the church, the Lord's return for His own. Oftentimes it becomes more than speculation; people become absolutely dogmatic about the subject. One of the most recent and widespread examples was the conviction that the Lord must return to the earth to establish His kingdom in 1988. The theory had something to do with the alignment of the stars and the planets. The date meant that a pre-Tribulation rapture had to occur by seven years earlier, or by 1981. Such a conviction was taught by some well-known and respected expositors of Bible prophecy. Thousands of Christians were convinced of the certainty of that prediction. But 1981 came and went, and the rapture did not occur.

It was time to reevaluate. Now the prognosticators said that there had been a slight miscalculation. It was the rapture that would occur in 1988, not the return of Christ to the earth in His second coming. Everything was now postponed seven years, but 1988 came and went as well, and still no rapture. We had run out of astronomical events, so the date-setters became silent—at least for a while. (A book called *88 Reasons Why the Rapture Will Come in 1988* also came and went with no effect.) Such expectations also arose during the Gulf War, and some people set dates again, with the same lack of results.

SPECULATIONS BRING REPROACH AND HARM FAITH

In addition to being just plain disobedient to the Lord's prohibition against date setting, the predictors bring the whole subject of prophecy into shame and disrepute. Unbelievers scoff at such shams, and professing Christians who do not believe in the rapture or the second coming hold such practices up for ridicule, lambaste prophetic teaching in general, and utterly throw the baby out with the bath water.

We simply must not allow ourselves to get caught up in the antiscriptural practice of attempting to set a date for the Lord's return. That activity may be comforting and encouraging to some for a while, and it may sell a great many books, but when the appointed day passes and nothing happens, disillusionment and confusion are left in the wake.

We must reconcile ourselves to the fact that God has given us a paradox in His consistent teaching about the second coming. His return for His own is imminent and could occur today or at any moment. But, for all we know, He could delay His return for many more years if He so chooses. We simply have to live our lives both ways—ready for His imminent return and, at the same time, planning ahead in case of His long delay. Such a double-visioned way of living is not easy, but that is scripturally the way the Lord has designed for His children to live.

THE PROPHETIC TIME CLOCK: IT CAN BE STARTED AGAIN ONLY AFTER THE RAPTURE AND THE BEGINNING OF THE TRIBULATION

Although no date is given for the rapture, when it has occurred the way will be paved for a definite timetable to be established. Some people hold that the rapture itself will start the seven-year period of the Tribulation, but that is not precisely the case. We must remember that the Tribulation is the Seventieth Week of Daniel, and it is tied in with the previous sixty-nine weeks:

> So you are to know and discern that from the issuing of a decree to restore and rebuild Jerusalem until Messiah the Prince there will be seven weeks and sixty-two weeks; it will be built again, with plaza and moat, even in times of

distress. Then after the sixty-two weeks the Messiah will be cut off and have nothing, and the people of the prince who is to come will destroy the city and the sanctuary. . . . And he will make a firm covenant with many for one week. (Daniel 9:25-27a)

The sixty-nine weeks ended when Messiah was cut off, at the time of His death on the cross. The prophetic clock stopped at the moment of His incomparable death and has never started again. During this "timeout," the centuries of the church age, which will not end until the rapture, are transpiring. But the rapture itself does not start the clock ticking again. The event that causes the ancient prophetic clock of Daniel to start up once more is the confirmation of the treaty between the evil prince, the Antichrist ("the prince who is to come"), and the "many," that is, the majority of Israel, whom this prophecy is about ("your people and . . . your holy city" [Daniel 9:24]). Daniel 9:27 mentions this treaty, or "covenant," an agreement for a period of seven years ("one week" in Daniel's parlance).

The contents of the treaty between the Antichrist and Israel are not disclosed, but it is reasonable to assume that the treaty involves a commitment by the Antichrist to guarantee Israel's territorial integrity. At any rate, when the treaty has been signed the entire well-defined schedule of the last seven years of human history before the Lord's return to the earth will be set into motion. The Tribulation itself is well marked with guideposts for those who believe the Scriptures: the treaty, the testimony of the 144,000 Jewish believers in Christ and that of the two witnesses, the desecration of the Temple, the persecution of Israel, the cataclysmic disasters all over the world, the war of Armageddon, the visible return of the Lord, and the establishment of His kingdom on the earth.

WE KNOW THE DESTINATION BUT NOT THE ROUTE

Such a well-defined schedule of events during the Tribulation is in contrast to the nebulous arrangement we have now during the church age, in which there is no certain date for the next event, the rapture. It is like having a map that is vague up to a certain point, but eventually becomes clear and detailed. The destination is known, but the route is murky, as if we see through a glass darkly, straining to make out what is on the other side.

Thus, through divine revelation we will know what will happen when it virtually starts happening. Our best estimate is that the Russian invasion of Israel will occur somewhere around the time of the rapture of the church. Both events happen at least seven years before the return of the Lord to the earth.

There are several views about how the rapture and the Russian invasion are related in time. It is conceivable that they could occur simultaneously, with the rapture of the church transpiring at the very moment the forces from the specified nations of Ezekiel's prophecy descend upon Israel.

On the other hand, it might also be speculated that the Russian invasion would take place shortly after the rapture. That is, in the worldwide confusion caused by the sudden removal of believers in Christ from the earth Russia and its allied nations would take advantage of the situation and bring about their attack on Israel.

Still another view is that there may be some gap in time between the rapture and the Russian invasion. During that period certain end-time events would be put in place, such as the final alignment of Russia and its allies, the preparation of the 144,000 Jewish Christian witnesses for the Tribulation, and the preparation of the Antichrist in the wings to step in with his program during the devastating aftermath of the Russian invasion. Even if there were such a gap, though, it would probably not be long, more a matter of months than years. With the church gone from the earth, little testimony of the Lord would be available in a critical time.

Once the rapture has occurred, believers simply will not be on earth any more. We will be in the presence of our Lord, observing all the ensuing events. Thus we have a sort of semidetached perspective of the Russian invasion of Israel and the Tribulation to follow. We know they are coming, and we see indications all around us that the stage is being set for those things to happen, and all that means a sooner rapture of the church. But we also know that before the Tribulation actually comes to pass, the Lord will remove His own from the earth. "Even so, come quickly, Lord Jesus."

So much has happened already. The dry bones of Israel are coming together in the land, just as Ezekiel predicts in the 36th and 37th chapters. The stage is set for the revival of the Roman Empire in Europe, and Russia, to the far north of Israel, has become an unpredictable superpower with enough nuclear bombs to destroy the world several times over.

But not all the pieces of the puzzle are yet in place. The economically and politically crippled former Soviet Union will have to sort out its new role in the world, and it is yet to be determined if that nation will pacify its restless internal states or if it will fall into anarchy and civil war.

How will Persia work itself into position as an ally of the Magog that arises out of the new Russia? Will Iraq, with its revived Babylon, join Iran to form the new Persia of the future? How will Saudi Arabia, the mogul of the oil wealthy Arab states, fit into the scenario? What about the immediate neighbors of Israel—Lebanon, Syria, Jordan, and Egypt? Will they be neutralized by Israel, either by some kind of treaty or by military action? What is the significance of the African states of Ethiopia and Libya? How can they be mobilized as participants in the initial invasion of the end time?

We know that the events will come to pass just as the prophet foresaw, and some of them appear to be possible in short order, but we can only speculate as to how it will all develop. Such speculation is what we endeavored to do in the earlier chapters; the suggested scenarios seem plausible, but they should be understood as mere educated speculations and nothing more. We believe the Lord allows speculation, and even encourages it, as long as it is understood that it is not equivalent to revelation.

THE NEWLY INCREASED LIKELIHOOD OF A SOON-COMING RUSSIAN INVASION OF ISRAEL AND THE ATTENDANT RAPTURE OF THE CHURCH

Are conditions better for the fulfillment of Ezekiel 38-39 than they were when we first published *The Coming Russian Invasion of Israel?* One thing is certain, we are definitely about twenty years nearer to its fulfillment.

To review briefly our updated material, there are some positives and some negatives in the current world scene with regard to the fulfillment of the prophecy of the war between Magog and Israel. On the one hand, the old Soviet Union is in apparent disarray politically and economically, but it is difficult to determine how it has fared militarily in the process. It still has vast thermonuclear capabilities and a huge army, but Russian weaponry and technology did not exactly distinguish themselves in the hands of the Iraqis during the Persian Gulf War. So, in some respects, Russia appears to have taken a step or two back from its monolithic stereotype as the fearsome atheistic power ready to swoop down upon Israel on behalf of its Arab client states.

But we use the term *appears* advisedly, because the Russian army and the KGB are still shrouded in secrecy. Who knows what could happen if that unhappy nation should fall into chaos and reactionary leaders should gain control of the levers of power and weaponry? Thus, we have to adopt a "wait and see" attitude toward Russia at this point.

In another way, one could speculate that there is an increased likelihood in today's world for the invasion of Israel by Russia and its selected allies. With the Gulf War, a precedent has been set for international settlement of territorial disputes. If there is sufficient agreement among the world powers, the United Nations can pass increasingly severe resolutions and sanctions against a nation that is perceived as being an aggressor and can ultimately go to war against such an aggressor with the full backing of international law.

That may not bode well for Israel's well-being, because most of the world perceives Israel as an aggressor occupying foreign territory on the West Bank. As we write, Israel is gradually being pushed into a corner by the United States and the Arab nations to agree to an international conference on the Middle East. One would hope that the various parties are sincere and that some kind of peace—at least a temporary peace—could be established. But if there are serious setbacks one could well imagine Russia's joining with allies like those specified by Ezekiel to take care of the "Israel problem" once and for all.

We trust that our readers will be enlightened and updated with regard to the significance of current events in the timetable of the "sure word of prophecy" and be prepared for whatever manner in which the Lord accomplishes what He has promised to do.

Although the world is being buffeted by the hurricane of events that blow down upon it, we who have trusted in the Savior can know that His coming for His own is nearer today than when we first believed. The authors of this book have had the privilege of meeting some of our reader friends already, and we look forward to meeting the rest of you personally some day, as the saying goes, here (on earth), there (in heaven), or in the air (at the rapture).

17
Millennium Update: 1999

It is truly remarkable how many updates of this book we have produced since 1973, when we first wrote the book. The basic message remains the same: the war of Gog and Magog described in Ezekiel 38-39 is on schedule as an event that will come to pass in the End Times. The only thing that continues to change is the stage setting from which this war will ultimately be launched. The following themes are the basis of our thesis:

1. The Gog and Magog war in Ezekiel is distinct from Armageddon and the Gog and Magog war described in Revelation 20.

2. This war involves certain distinct nations (Magog, Persia, Ethiopia and Libya), which is different from the war of Armageddon, with all the nations of the earth participating. There is no nation today named Magog, so its identification has caused much speculation among Bible interpreters. Our understanding is that the Scriptural evidence points toward the nation to the far north of Israel that we know as Russia.

When we first wrote the book, Russia was a dominant part of the Soviet Union. Since then, the Soviet Union has collapsed into smaller autonomous units, but Russia remains dominant, and also is the repository for huge quantities of nuclear and military weapons. Russia also continues to maintain close ties with Persia (Iran) and the Moslem world, overtly and covertly sending military supplies and advice to them. At the same time, millions of Jews have left Russia in order to emigrate to Israel.

3. The timing of the Ezekiel war is not precisely spelled out in the Scriptures, and reliable interpreters have differed over this question. But the evidence strongly suggests to us that the war will occur near the beginning of the 70th Week of Daniel, also known as the seven-year Tribulation. In fact, this war may occur sometime before the Tribulation, and may be in close proximity with the Rapture of the Church. Much of this about timing is speculation, but is based on logical deductions from the information that is given in the Word about the Gog and Magog war, the Tribulation and the Rapture.

4. In the scenario we suggest, the Rapture of the Church, which is imminent and can occur at any moment, might well occur just before the Gog and Magog war. With the massive departure of believers in Christ, governments will be destabilized. Russia will be tempted, with its allied nations, to attack Israel. It may be that the attackers will hold America and the West at bay by threatening to detonate several "suitcase" nuclear bombs if they interfere with their invasion of Israel. Whatever the reason, the invading armies are allowed by the other nations to make their powerful attack "as a cloud" against Israel.

5. Once the invasion begins, there will be an enormous outpouring of supernatural power, including earthquakes and fiery hail. The invading army will be demolished as it attempts to conquer Israel. They will fall in the mountains and valleys of Israel. It is interesting, by the way, that the

Lord consistently calls the land to which the Jewish people have been restored in the last days "Israel." It is not called "Palestine" or any other name. Israel is the only name that God recognizes for His Holy Land, and that is true throughout the Scriptures.

6. The armies of Russia, Persia, Ethiopia and Libya will have a 5/6 (83%) casualty rate, with only a few of the soldiers surviving to return home to tell the awesome story. Israel will be the victor, and the God of Abraham, Isaac and Jacob will receive the glory for defeating these latter-day enemies.

7. In our proposed scenario, after the dust of Gog and Magog settles, a huge delusion will engulf the nation of Israel and the entire world. Into this chaos steps the Antichrist, who, we suggest, will claim to be the one who has delivered Israel, and has a program to remove the chaos and bring peace and prosperity to the world. The "many" of Israel will be deceived, and will endorse the "covenant" with the Man of Sin, thus beginning the events of the Tribulation, leading up to the Second Coming of Christ to the earth.

8. All of the above events are described in the Scriptures. The precise order may or may not be as we have suggested above. However, we are convinced that, when Ezekiel's prophecy is fulfilled, those who believe the Bible at that time will say that everything is done precisely as he and the other Bible prophets foretold.

9. The challenge to Bible-believing Christians today is to continue proclaiming the Gospel to Jews and Gentiles, continue edifying the Body of the Lord, and continue to await eagerly the Rapture of the Church, when He will receive us unto Himself. Even so, come quickly, Lord Jesus.

Changes In Russia

Since our last update of this book on the upcoming invasion of Israel by Russia and its Moslem associate nations, a number of significant events have occurred. The prophecy of Ezekiel has not changed and remains forever true until it is literally fulfilled. When it comes to pass, everyone who believes the Bible will affirm that everything Ezekiel prophesied came to pass precisely.

What has changed is the situation in a number of the key players in the coming invasion described by Ezekiel, namely Russia (Magog), Iran (Persia), Ethiopia (Cush) and Libya (Put). Even though the Iron Curtain had fallen by the time of our last update in 1992, additional changes have taken place in Russia since then. Among the changes in Russia internally that are significant are the growth of anti-Semitism, and an enormous emigration of Jewish people from Russia to Israel. External changes are the relations Russia has developed during the last few years with Iran and Iraq.

GROWING RUSSIAN ANTI-SEMITISM

Anti-Jewish attitudes have always been widespread throughout Russia. During the reign of the Czars there were many "pogroms," or violent persecutions, against the Jews. Ghettos became common in the land, and Jewish people were herded into these restricted quarters in hundreds of cities. Strangely enough, it was Communism that gave the Jewish people hope of rescue from the anti-Semitism that had dominated Russia for so many centuries. The non-religious communist government at least papered over the long-held animosities, and made it possible for Jewish people to rise to higher levels of administration and management throughout the system.

To say the least, Russia was not prepared for the collapse of Communism and the Soviet Union at the beginning of this decade. To the outward observer, Russia has adopted many of the worst aspects of democracy and capitalism, such as political cronyism and racketeering. Many of the Jews of Russia were involved in the finance and banking industry, and when those institutions failed, the Jewish managers caught much of the blame. As has often been the case, the Jewish populace became a scapegoat for the economic problems and ultimate collapse experienced by Russia.

An intensive study of this problem has been done in a book by Semyon Reznik, entitled *The Nazification of Russia: Anti-Semitism in the Post-Soviet Era.* For the first time since the Czars ruled Russia, Jews were openly attacked, and various organizations were formed that have attempted to blame the economic turmoil on the Jews. In addition, some of the political leaders surfacing in Russia have expressed strong anti-Jewish sentiments. All of these developments did not bode well for the Jewish people in Russia.

MASSIVE EMIGRATION TO ISRAEL

As a result of this revived anti-Semitism, as well as the general upheavals in the country, the emigration of Jews out of Russia to Israel increased dramatically from a trickle, to a stream, to a veritable flood amounting to about two million during the course of the '90s. Absorbing all these people became a huge problem in Israel, and the efforts to resettle them have been Herculean (or is it better to say Samsonian?). The saga of this doubling of Israel's Jewish population over such a short period of time has been the subject of numerous studies. Recently, there was a photographic display showing the pictures of the emigrants from Russia and other countries to modern Israel. Below is a report on the display published on the Internet:

"Today's Israelis," through Jan. 29, at SPAS Gallery
"Today's Israelis — A Country in Transition" is a photographic documentary by Bruce Bennett, a Rochester-based photographer and RIT alumnus, on view in January in the School of Photographic Arts and Sciences Gallery. The documentary illustrates the migration to Israel of Jews from Africa, Morocco and Russia over a period of seven years. The work explores Israel's changing identity and the journey of that country toward tolerance, patience and understanding.

"Israel welcomes the migration of the Jewish populace," says Bennett. "For recently arrived African, Russian and Moroccan Jews, the pilgrimage to Israel has been a rebirth. With immense measures of courage and joy, they embrace the opportunity to live in peace… 'Today's Israelis' offers my deep appreciation for the history and circumstances surrounding the transition of these ancient cultures."

The huge influx of people has caused considerable strain on the young, modern country of Israel, and many of the immigrants, including the Russians, have had difficulty obtaining gainful employment. Some highly trained doctors and musicians found themselves in menial jobs in their adopted land, which made it very difficult for them to adapt. Also, much of the impulse to expand into the West Bank and create new "settlements" came from the increase in population. That developed into considerable political pressure on Israel to cease the construction of the new settlements from the Palestinians, the UN and even the U.S. government. However, the expansion of the population had at least one positive result: it has given more strength, cultural diversity and stability to Israel.

CONTINUING RUSSIAN MILITARY POWER

It is not just the internal conditions in Russia that cause concern. It is also the international relations that the old communist capital state has forged. They show that its movement toward the events described in Ezekiel have not abated. As long as the massive Soviet Union existed at the height of the Cold War, its role as an enemy of Israel and a supplier of Israel's neighboring antagonists appeared to qualify it as the quintessential Magog. However, when the Soviet Union fell apart, many Bible students began to question if its Russian core would still qualify as the Magog of Ezekiel.

Subsequent events in the intervening years have borne out that the new Russia is every bit as potentially dangerous to world stability in general, and the Middle East in particular, as the old Soviet Union. Granted, Russia alone does not have the massive military establishment or the financial clout that the old hegemony had, but it does still have enough presence to cause considerable troubles on the world scene. There are still hundreds of nuclear missiles in silos throughout Russia. We have been told that these missiles are no longer targeted, but they could be re-targeted with little effort, so it is difficult to feel too relieved about the disarmament conditions.

Russia also has ideological links with China, which is no small power on today's world scene. While China is regarded as a major power in the War of Armageddon ("the King of the East"), it is able to extend military assistance and capability to Russia for Ezekiel's invasion earlier. Journalist Christopher Ruddy has done some investigation of the current military power of Russia and its compatriot China, and what Russia is doing in military terms. The February 9, 1999, edition of NewsMax.com's Internet Vortex — the newsletter of investigative reporting — leads with an article about Ruddy's story, entitled "Russia and China Prepare for War."

Ruddy details major developments in China and Russia

that appear as war preparations — developments that have gone unnoticed by the major media: China and Russia have openly entered into an alliance — an alliance intended, by their own admission, to challenge the dominance of the United States. Both countries have been moving troops off their shared borders, as military cooperation has been stepped up. This new strategic alliance may be among the most momentous acts of the twentieth century — despite the scant attention the media has paid to it.

Russia's war machine continues to expand. Contrary to popular notion, Russia did not disband its military-industrial complex. Ruddy shreds the myth that Russia is a weak country. In recent months Russia has deployed a regiment of TOPOL-M intercontinental ballistic missiles, weapons more sophisticated than anything in the American arsenal. This past fall, President Yeltsin commissioned *Peter the Great,* the largest ballistic missile cruiser ever built. The war machine also turned out a new stealth bomber, and Russia continues to build new submarines at rates equal to the days of the Cold War.

While these and many other ominous developments take place in Russia and China, the Clinton administration has slashed defense spending and reduced America's military readiness. No longer can America fight a war on one front, let alone two. The Clinton administration has also destroyed two-thirds of America's nuclear arsenal, making Russia the nation with the largest nuclear arsenal. Never has America been so vulnerable. With Russia's economic collapse, never has the fate of world peace been so precarious.

In Internet Vortex, Ruddy writes about Jeffrey Nyquist, an independent researcher on Russia, who predicted that Russia's economy would collapse. Nyquist says Russia has been taking 11 steps that would allow them to launch a surprise nuclear attack against the United States.

Nyquist pieces together information — from published, reputable sources — that suggest a war scenario. These include:

Russia has been moving its strategic nuclear warheads onto their naval ships — where they will be less vulnerable to an American counterstrike. Russia has put its nuclear arsenal under joint command — a judicious move in an offensive war.

Russia has been hoarding food, gold and oil. Russia's famine is questionable, and she has been slaughtering her livestock at unprecedented rates. Russia has regularly put its nuclear forces on high alert — which has the effect of fooling America's early warning systems. Russia's military has been engaging [in] numerous mock attacks against the United States — these exercises have included Russia's Strategic Rocket Forces, bombers and naval forces. Nyquist argues that many factors may be leading Russia's military to consider a war option.

Notable is the "tripwire" of Y2K. Just this month, Russia's military authorities admitted Y2K will have catastrophic effects on its nuclear arsenal. This admission reverses previous claims that Russia would not be affected by Y2K. For months, Nyquist has been pointing to the Y2K problem, noting that Russia's military is faced with a problem: either the Russian military uses their nuclear weapons before the year 2000 or they risk losing them for a period of time.

One leading expert on Russia, Colonel Stainslav Lunev, agrees with Nyquist's concerns. Lunev, a former GRU officer, in a video interview with NewsMax.com, warns that Y2K may be a tripwire for war.

In the coming edition of Internet Vortex, due out in mid-February, Jeffrey Nyquist explores recent developments in Russia and China that continue a disturbing pattern of war preparations.

© 1998, NewsMax.com Original Site Design by David Grumm / HTML by Luke Kelly

There are also rumors about dozens of "suitcase nuclear bombs" that the Russian military establishment has "lost," and could well be in the hands of terrorist groups determined to destabilize the world. It is possible these portable bombs do exist, and that they are still under the control of the Russian military. In the scenario of the Gog and Magog war, some have speculated that when Russia and its collaborating nations are ready to attack, they may attempt to hold the West at bay by threatening to unleash some of these portable bombs in the major cities.

RUSSIAN RELATIONS WITH IRAN

Furthermore, the foreign relations of Russia have continued in the post-Soviet era much the same as they did before. For instance, Russia has long had a friendly relationship with Iran. Military and intelligence figures were constantly going back and forth between the two countries during the Cold War, and they continue today. Nuclear assistance has flowed from Russia to Iran, and the "bear of the north" is currently assisting Iran with a new atomic energy plant, as *The Times* of India reported:

> Russia, Iran Sign Nuclear Accord
> Thursday 26 November 1998
> TEHRAN: Iran and Russia signed a cooperation accord to speed up completion of a controversial Iranian nuclear reactor on the Gulf and study possible joint development of other power plants.

Russia has agreed that completion of the first phase of the Bushehr Plant would be brought forward by three months, while a joint committee will look at financial issues involving the second phase of the project, state radio reported on Tuesday.

Under the accord signed at the end of a visit here by Russian Atomic Energy Minister Yevgeny Adamov, the two countries also agreed in principle to study the construction of more power plants in Iran, the radio said. Qolam-Reza Agazadeh, the head of Iran's atomic energy organization, said that the $778 million project would be completed on time "despite external political pressures," according to the official IRNA news agency. Adamov also said on Monday that his country was determined to continue its nuclear cooperation with Iran. (AFP)

As has been seen in India, Pakistan and North Korea, it is not difficult to move from a nuclear power plant to primitive nuclear weapons. There are rumors that Iran already has possession of a nuclear bomb. If they do not, it will probably only be a matter of time before Iran will have this capability, and they have their patron Russia to thank for it. Iran, of course, is the Persia of the Bible, and the fact that Russia and Iran are working closely together in these matters could pave the way for them to forge an attack against Israel. This is the kind of cooperation indicated by the prophecy in Ezekiel that will lead to a joint invasion.

THE RUSSIA-IRAQ CONNECTION

In the current geopolitical map, Iran (Persia) and Iraq are separate countries. Indeed, they were actually at war with one another throughout most of the 1980s. However, think of the condition of Iran at the time Ezekiel wrote his inspired book. It was a subordinate district to the nation of Babylon (Iraq), and was actually under the control of Babylon. When Persia conquered Babylon near the close of Daniel's life and ministry, Babylon was incorporated within (Medo) Persia. It is possible that, when the war of Gog and Magog is fulfilled, Iran and Iraq may be consolidated again. Even though they represent opposing denominations within the Moslem religion, they are, after all, both Moslem countries. There is some evidence of a rapprochement between the two countries, and their consolidation is not unthinkable.

At any rate, Russia is considered even more of a protector of Iraq than it is of Iran. For years Russia has been an outspoken advocate of Iraq and Saddam Hussein throughout all of the controversy with the United Nations, the

United States and Britain over the inspections of weapons of mass destruction. National Public Radio News reported on how Russia may have been one of the primary sources of biological weapons to Iraq:

> Russia/Iraq Connection?
> February 12, 1998—Responding to congressional calls for a clearer policy on Iraq, U.S. Secretary of State Madeleine Albright said today the long-range aim is to remove Saddam Hussein as president, but not with American combat troops.
> U.S. Defense Secretary William Cohen is meeting with Russian officials in Moscow, after completing a tour of the Middle East. Cohen says he will not try to change Moscow's opposition to a military strike on Iraq, but the topic was high on the agenda. Russia has taken the lead in efforts to end the standoff between Iraq and the United Nations, diplomatically.
> But a report in this morning's *Washington Post* suggests Russia may have other reasons to side with Iraq. According to the report, the UN is investigating whether Russia may have sold Iraq some of the equipment it would need to make biological weapons. From Moscow, NPR's Andy Bowers reports.
> The suggestion is that Russia is resisting the UN inspections in Iraq because their complicity in providing some of the biological weapons to Saddam Hussein might be exposed. That might help to explain why Russia has been so adamant in protecting Iraq in this persistent struggle.

At any rate, when Ezekiel predicts that Magog will coordinate with Persia in the End Times invasion of Israel, it is possible that all of that Mesopotamian region is meant, including Iran and Iraq. Russia's intimate involvement with both of these countries culturally and militarily may well be a harbinger of things to come.

Libya And Ethiopia: Potential Invaders Of Israel

Libya has long been known as an enemy of Israel, and Col. Kadafi's hatred of the Jewish nation has been legendary for at least two decades. Libya has a well-earned reputation for the training and exporting of terrorists. The Lockerbie, Scotland, bombing of the TWA flight in the 1980s has still not been resolved, even though official charges have been made against terrorists who have been aided, abetted and harbored by Libya. However, there is nothing particularly new about Libya since our last update at the beginning of this decade. It remains a potential ally of Russia in its prophesied attack on Israel.

Ethiopia, on the other hand, is something of an enigma. The country known as Ethiopia today has a tragic history during this century. It has an ancient relationship with Israel that claims to go back to the days of King Solomon and the Queen of Sheba. There is even a long, though highly questionable, tradition that Ethiopia became the repository for the missing Ark of the Covenant from ancient times to the present. The venerable Haile Selassie actually claimed to be a descendant of King Solomon, and called himself the "Lion of the Tribe of Judah." All of this may be very questionable, but it demonstrates the historical attachment Ethiopia has had toward Israel and the Jewish people. For some years, Ethiopia was one of few countries in Africa that had direct commercial flight connections with Israel.

Of course, the most direct connection of all with the Holy Land is the phenomenon of Falashas. These remarkable Jewish people, black Ethiopians all, have come to Israel in massive airlifts in the past decade or so. They had been separated from the rest of the Jewish people for some three thousand years! Their doctrines go back only to the Pentateuch, or the first five books of the Bible, since they were away when the prophecy, Psalms, etc. were issued.

But their Judaism is unquestioned, and Israel became the first nation in the world to bring black Africans into their culture, not as slaves, but as first class citizens.

The Falashas tended to live in peace in the Ethiopia of Selassie. There has been considerable turmoil, however, in Ethiopia in more recent times. The Communists managed to take over the country, and the nation has been on a roller coaster ride economically and politically during the past couple of decades. It is not particularly clear at this time how Ethiopia, as such, would be drawn into the conflict described in Ezekiel.

It should be noted, though, that modern Ethiopia is only part of what was understood as Ethiopia in Ezekiel's time. Theologian Charles Ryrie explains that at that time Ethiopia included the area south of Egypt, which is known as Sudan now:

> Other allies will include Persia (modern Iran), Ethiopia (northern Sudan), Libya, Gomer (probably the eastern part of Turkey and the Ukraine), and the House of Togarmah (the part of Turkey near the Syrian border). *Charles F. Ryrie Study Bible,* p. 1197.

If Ezekiel's prophecy includes Sudan, one can readily see how it could well develop into an enemy of Israel, and join the other selected nations in the attack in the End Times. The Moslems tend to look at the Jews and Christians in the same camp as fellow infidels. Whatever Jews may have lived in Sudan have apparently left, but there is a relatively large population of Christians in the country. They have been suffering much persecution from the Moslem majority for some time. The following reports about the persecution of Christians in Sudan have been posted on the Internet:

SUDANESE CHRISTIANS PERSECUTED BY MUSLIMS FROM THE NORTH

Sudan: United churches prevent bloodbath in Rank. We have just heard that united action by churches in Rank, an isolated area in the northernmost part of southern Sudan, about 12 hours by bus from Khartoum, prevented a massacre in February 1996. The Sudanese government is continuing its attempts to turn the country into a Moslem state; one of their strategies is to 'convert' pupils between 6 and 12 years old in school. The region's government representative asked the churches to open their doors for Islamic teaching. When the churches refused, he threatened to use force, to which they replied 'So, use force.' When the official arrived with the army, he found the members of all the local churches around the building. Because a military action would have caused a bloodbath, he thought better of it and withdrew after arresting some of the leaders, who were released a week later. The Rank churches celebrated this as a great victory in the face of the permanent persecution in Sudan.

Source: DAWN Friday Fax, 2-28-96

Remain steadfast in prayer for believers in southern Sudan. An estimated 3 million people — many of them Christians — have died since the military junta in Khartoum declared 'holy war' against non-Muslims in 1992. One news service reports: "Soldiers plunder the villages, rape the women and torture or kill the men. Some victims have been burned alive, while others had their ears or genital organs amputated. More than 10,000 women and children have been kidnapped and sold as slaves. Lift God's suffering children to the throne of grace."

(Advance is Copyright © 1996, Kainos Press)

Sudan is perhaps the worst violator. Its Islamic government has engaged in a policy of forcible conversion. Many of the black Sudanese in the southern part of the country (the north is Arab) have resisted conversion, in many cases because of adherence to Christianity (a criminal act under Sudanese law). As punishment, the Sudanese government has denied food and medicine to Christians in famine areas and has sold thousands of Christian children — some as young as 6 — into slavery. (Mona Cherin article)

Hold up believers in Sudan, where forces sponsored by the Islamic military government continue to use torture, kidnapping, slavery and rape to oppress Christians and animists in the south. The United Nations Human Rights Commission will discuss claims that young children have been stolen and forced into Islamic re-education programs, older boys pressed into military service and girls imprisoned as sex slaves. Ask God to comfort his oppressed children and to deliver them from injustice. Pray that God would reveal himself to Muslim power broker Hassan Turabi.

The Vatican accused Sudan's government in February of torturing a priest and a student, forcing them to confess to recruiting rebels and plotting bombing attacks. Christians and animists in southern Sudan have struggled against northern Muslim oppression since 1983, suffering kidnapping, forced military service and even crucifixion. Ask God to strengthen his people and deliver them from evil. (Advance is Copyright © 1996, Kainos Press)

Voice of the Martyrs: In Sudan: Christians have been starved and killed, pastors have been crucified (literally), and the children of Christians have been kidnapped into slavery.

Voice of America reports: Sudan Appeal (L-O) — [11-Jul-96 2:08 PM EDT (1808 UTC)] A U.N. food agency has urgently appealed to the government of Sudan to allow large aircraft to drop food into rebel-held areas in the southern region, engulfed in civil war for the past 13 years. The Executive Director of the World Food Program made a special trip to New York to talk (Thursday) about impending starvation in the area. (Correspondent Elaine Johanson reports.)

The above reports are certainly a tragic litany of persecution of believers in Christ on a scale that reminds us of the persecution in the worst days of the Roman Empire. In truth, more people have been killed in the name of Christ in this century than in any century since the Lord came, mostly at the hands of the Moslems and the Communists. Sudan has entered into this awful history with a vengeance.

→ Christians and Jews are taken together in Moslem thinking as infidels or idolaters. The "people of the book," the Jews and the Christians who read the Bible, are separated in Islamic thought from the secular peoples. The animosity toward Christians is therefore representative of the very similar animosity toward Israel. We believe that it is very reasonable to place Sudan in this invasion, cooperating with the other powers who attack Israel. It is not difficult to imagine Sudan, as part of the ancient Ethiopia, cooperating with the Gog and Magog invasion of Israel.

THE INTERNATIONAL BIAS AGAINST ISRAEL

One thing that the Ezekiel Gog and Magog war and the War of Armageddon have in common is an intense animosity against the Lord God and Israel. If the Gog and Magog war were to occur today, it would seem that kind of animosity is already in place. It became evident as long ago as the Yom Kippur War in 1973. When Israel was attacked then from the north and the south and was in dire straits with the possibility that the nation could have been destroyed, only the United States and Holland came to Israel's aid. From that time, the United Nations, an international governmental coalition, and the media have all joined together in a systematic propaganda attack on Israel. Sometimes it has been subtle, sometimes it has been overt, but it has been persistent. Co-author Zola Levitt comments in the upcoming "Foreshadows of Wrath":

> Media attention is what makes a prime minister or a nation famous or infamous in today's world, and for some reason (known only to Scripture), Israel gets much more than

its share of it. While a handful of reporters cover European capitals, there are 400 newsmen, TV commentators and the like in Jerusalem every day! While entire revolutions take place in countries ten times Israel's size with minor media coverage, CNN virtually stops its news day to report that the orthodox and the secular Jewish people are arguing again on some Israeli street.

The Dallas Morning News, a reliable critic of Israel along with so many of its sister newspapers in this country, ran a picture of so-called strife while covering some neighborhood disagreement in the Holy Land in which there were zero casualties. The front page story was accompanied by a huge photograph of the factions that were arguing. On page 13 of the same paper it recorded seven murders over the same weekend in Dallas.

The New York Times, our "newspaper of record," keeps up a steady drumbeat of criticism of this allied democracy no matter what else in the world is happening. I would think that if a world war broke out, the Times editor would order his reporters to keep a front page space open for its usual Israel coverage whatever else might be happening.

We must keep in mind that the media are not some public service but simply profit-making businesses which charge substantial fees for the coverage provided. In previous editions in this series of books, I have pointed out that the media are likely supported by petrodollars since makers of oil-based products buy a great deal of advertising. If the makers of cars, cosmetics, gasolines and so forth are not pleased with the sort of coverage that they receive in the media — if it does not somehow support Arab oil interests — then they possibly buy less advertising space. And so we have a profit-making business covering an ordinary day-to-day life situation in Israel in a most negative and provocative way for reasons of greater profits.

This kind of animosity toward Israel in its struggle for existence and its struggle with the Palestinians has dominated the world media, the deliberations in the United Nations, and the policies of the country that is supposed to be Israel's best friend, the U.S. The only groups in the U.S. that have consistently supported Israel are a majority of the Jewish people and a sizeable minority of evangelical Christians who believe in the future of Israel, and who look forward to the Second Coming of Christ.

If the Rapture of the Church were to occur in the near future, the believers in the Lord Jesus would be taken out of the world. This would leave only the substantial Jewish population in the country and the Gentiles who only give the Bible lip service. The U. S. and Western civilization would be destabilized and vulnerable to attack. The Jewish people might consider that they faced only persecution in the nations, and many would head for Israel. Russia and its allied nations might consider this to be a prime time to attack Israel with impunity.

Such is the possible scenario that might lead to the Gog and Magog war. The exact time of its occurrence is not revealed, but the fact that it will occur is certain. The prophecies of the Word of God always come to pass in His good time, without fail.